MANUAL

OF

THE JARVES COLLECTION

OF

Early Italian Pictures

Deposited in the Galleries of the Yale School of Fine Arts.

New-Haven:
PUBLISHED BY YALE COLLEGE.
1868.

UMBRIAN AND SIENESE SCHOOLS — VENITIAN SCHOOL

1200 — 1225 — 1250 — 1275 — 1300 — 1325 — 1350 — 1375 — 1400 — 1425 — 1450 — 1475 — 1500 — 1525 — 1550 — 1575 — 1600 — 1625 — 1650

Paolo Caliari (Veronese)
* Jacopo Robusti (Tintoretto)
Jacopo del Ponte
Margaritone da Arezzo
Paris Bordone
Duccio da Siena
Sebastiano del Piombo
Simone Martini
* Tiziano Vecellio
Giorgione
Basaiti
Spinello Aretino
* Vittore Carpaccio
Giovanni Bellini
Gentile da Fabriano
Sassetta
Giunta da Pisa
Sano di Pietro
Giovanni di Paolo
Matteo da Siena
Luca Signorelli
Vanucci (Perugino)
Raibolini (Francia)
Piero della Francesca
Pinturicchio
Razzi (Sodoma)
* Raffaello Santi
Lo Spagna
Venusti
Pietro Cavallini
Giorgio Vasari
Altissimo
Pontormo
Andrea del Sarto
Ridolfo del Ghirlandajo
Franciabigio
Albertinelli
* Michelangelo Buonarotti
Fra Bartolomeo
Piero di Cosimo
Filippino Lippi
Lorenzo di Credi
Dominico del Ghirlandajo
Sandro Botticelli
Pietro Pollajuolo
Cosimo Roselli
Antonio Pollajuolo
Verocchio
* Guercino
Benozzo Gozzoli
Neri di Bicci
Domenichino
Fra Diamante
Guido Reni
Fra Filippo Lippi
Agostino Caracci
Dello Delli
* Ludovico Caracci
Masolino da Panicale
Masaccio
Paolo Ucelli
Andrea del Castagno
Fra Angelico
Lorenzo di Bicci
Antonio Veneziano
Giottino
Jacopo Da Casentino
Cotignola (Zaganelli)
Agnolo Gaddi
* Bernadino Luino
Puccio Capana
Orcagna
* Leonardo da Vinci
Taddeo Gaddi
Mantegna
Giotto di Bondone
Squarcione
Giovanni Cimabue

1200 — 1225 — 1250 — 1275 — 1300 — 1325 — 1350 — 1375 — 1400 — 1425 — 1450 — 1475 — 1500 — 1525 — 1550 — 1575 — 1600 — 1625 — 1650

* denotes Painters not represented in the Jarves Collection.

FLORENTINE SCHOOL — SCHOOLS OF LOMBARDY — BOLOGNESE SCHOOL

Am. Photo-Lithographic Co. N.Y. (Osborne's Process.)

MANUAL

OF THE

JARVES COLLECTION.

MANUAL

OF THE

JARVES COLLECTION

OF

EARLY ITALIAN PICTURES,

DEPOSITED IN THE GALLERIES OF THE YALE SCHOOL OF FINE ARTS.

BEING A

CATALOGUE, WITH DESCRIPTIONS OF THE PICTURES CONTAINED IN THAT COLLECTION, WITH BIOGRAPHICAL NOTICES OF ARTISTS AND AN INTRODUCTORY ESSAY, THE WHOLE FORMING A BRIEF

GUIDE TO THE STUDY OF EARLY CHRISTIAN ART.

BY

RUSSELL STURGIS, JR.

NEW-HAVEN:
PUBLISHED BY YALE COLLEGE.

1868.

NOTE.

The Yale School of the Fine Arts is a department of Yale College, which was instituted by the munificence of the late Augustus Russell Street, of New-Haven, who erected upon the College square a large and costly building containing galleries adapted to the exhibition of paintings, sculpture, and other works of art, and rooms designed for the studios of artists, and for the instruction of classes. He also made some provision, not yet available, for the endowment of the school.

The building was opened in 1866, and in the following summer a collection of modern pictures, by European and American artists, was exhibited in the galleries.

The pictures constituting the "Jarves Collection" were deposited in the gallery at the close of the year 1867, with an agreement that they should remain for a period of three years. It is hoped that before this time shall expire, the collection may be permanently secured.

The council who are in charge of the school are the President of the College, Rev. Dr. Woolsey, *ex officio*, Professor S. F. B. Morse, *perpetual member*, and Messrs. Daniel Huntington, Donald G. Mitchell, Edward E. Salisbury, and Noah Porter.

INTRODUCTORY ESSAY.

COLLECTION OF EARLY ITALIAN PICTURES.

The Jarves Collection, as it now appears in one of the galleries of the Yale School of the Fine Arts, is the partial result of an undertaking which was begun twelve years ago, and which is not yet abandoned. The complete success of this undertaking would be to secure for permanent free exhibition in America a gallery of pictures which should sufficiently represent Italian painting, from the eleventh to the beginning of the seventeenth century. The work was begun at a fortunate time. It would be very difficult now, and it will not be less difficult at any future time, to form another collection of an hundred and twenty pictures which should at all approach this one in value. It will not be easy, under the most favorable conditions, and with the present collection secured already, to complete the chronological sequence of pictures, nor to get together in the Jarves gallery pictures representative of all the Italian schools of painting. But important additions are possible; and every such addition will greatly increase the historical and educational value of the collection, because of the light which each work of art casts upon all other works of art with which it is in relation.

The study of early Italian painting can be pursued in galleries of pictures only under certain limitations. The principal work of the greatest painters was done altogether upon walls, either directly upon the plaster in fresco or distemper, or upon panels or stretched canvas, not meant for removal, and as yet unremoved. The Jarves gallery shares with all other picture-galleries the disadvantage that it has only small pictures to represent painters whose full strength was called forth only for large and immovable ones, — for the painting of the vaulted roofs of churches, the vast interior wall-spaces of civic and religious buildings, and the stuccoed exterior walls of later times. The work of Giotto cannot be critically studied in any gallery of Europe; but only in such buildings as the Arena Chapel at Padua, the Incoronata at Naples, the conventual church at Assisi, and the Campo Santo at Pisa. Tintoretto cannot be judged in the picture-galleries, even in those of Venice, where are so many large pictures by him; but only in the Scuola di San Rocco and in the Ducal Palace. The gallery-pictures ascribed to these great men, even when authentic and in good condition, are their slighter works; often delightful and full of character, and then partially representative of the artist, as a sonnet is of Dante or a song of Shakespeare; often comparatively mannered and feeble, and then either by pupils wholly or in part, or else job-work, done in the way of business, in a wearied and half-hearted manner. This is true especially of the painters before the time of Fra Angelico; Cimabue, Duccio, Simone Martini, Orcagna, and their contemporaries, are, in general, as inadequately represented by gallery-pictures as Giotto himself. Even those artists who are the most favorably known by small and transportable pictures, as, notably, Fra Angelico, must be studied in fresco as well. And in the case of one great artist, at least, no easel-pictures whatever are known to exist; of the three which are ascribed to Michelangelo, two in Florence and one in England, two are given up by all the critics, and the authenticity of the third is very doubtful.

If it is to be conceded, then, that galleries of Italian pictures are, relatively to the whole mass of Italian painting, of inferior importance, it is to be remembered that they are of enormous importance as compared with the paintings of other times and other schools. The very fact that the painters worked generally at large paintings of permanent and monumental character, has given to these smaller works a value which the works of other and differently trained artists have never equalled. The elevation of soul and the religious and poetic fervor of a great artist at work upon church walls, producing paintings of generally understood subjects, to remain permanently for all the world to see, will probably exceed the possible inspiration and enthusiasm of an equal man painting small pictures, to be sold to he knows not whom, and to be locked up he knows not where. Art could hardly have progressed, in a century, from Giotto to

Masaccio, if the Italians had asked for cabinet pictures, or for transportable paintings of even large size, instead of mosaics, frescoes, and huge altar-pieces. But there was nothing then of the too common modern feeling toward a picture, as toward an expensive piece of furniture or wall-hanging. Even the minor works of the time partook of the general character of the larger, and had something of their immovableness. Thus an altar-piece, like No. 16 of this catalogue, or even a smaller one, like No. 37, was as permanently fixed above its altar as Duccio's great work at Siena; a tabernacle-picture, of which class of works our collection has many specimens, though more apt to be moved, had its definitely fixed place in the private oratory, or where, in a retired place, a room-corner was reserved for the reading-desk and for prayer. Art could not become nor continue trivial when, in addition to the solemnity of its usual subjects, and to the character of the people strongly disposed toward it, the works to which the artists gave their best strength were of general, almost national concern. And not only this, design also was necessarily more free and color composition more noble and solemn, where men worked on a large scale, than could be the case, even if other things were equal, where minute work is the universal rule.

The question of authenticity is one that is often of importance in the study of early pictures. There are very few works of art, especially among those which can be gathered into galleries, of which a complete documentary history exists; and wherever it is wanting, some uncertainty in regard to the picture may be allowed to exist. Tradition, signature, and internal evidence are the three means which are usually at our disposal; and of these the last is the most generally applicable, and is capable of being the most accurate. The agreement, in the case of one picture, of any two of these three kinds of evidence may be considered final; but in many cases internal evidence is all there is upon which to found a judgment.

The criticism of pictures has been greatly developed within the last fifteen years; its rules are more definite, and are known to a larger number of persons; moreover, the number of facts serving as material for judgment has been greatly increased, and it is possible to ascertain, by internal evidence alone, the authorship of a great number of works of art which has remained unknown, or has been falsely stated. The catalogues of some great public collections in Europe are still disfigured by mistaken assertions as to the authorship of pictures—assertions which all competent critics pronounce erroneous, but which the guardians of the collections, interested in maintaining a prestige even though founded upon error, have not yet been induced to remove. Such mistakes ought to be of very rare occurrence now, for the means exist of correct decision in the majority of cases; and it is easy and not unusual to indicate the existence and the degree of uncertainty in all cases where the evidence is insufficient.

It is to be observed that many painters, and among

them some of the best, are known to us principally through their pictures. The artists of quiet life and constant and peaceful labor, about whom few anecdotes are told, who excited little attention during their lives by eccentricity and personal display, were those who, of the painters before Raphael at least, have left us the greatest number of the most valuable pictures. The few exceptions are the men of pre-eminent genius and unquestioned leadership,—notably, Giotto. Of men somewhat less prominent, of whom we know little except through their remaining works, some are known by wall-pictures in all parts of Italy, and easel-pictures all over Europe; some, like Masaccio, are known by a few important wall-pictures only, the easel-pictures ascribed to them being of doubtful authenticity and inferior in power; some, like Gentile da Fabriano, are represented by easel-pictures only, and by but few of these, all else having perished. It is plain that internal evidence is very differently offered in these different cases. And there are names which are little more than names; an extreme instance of this is Giottino. It cannot be shown that all the works generally classed under his name are by the same man. It is probable that several Giotteschi, of similar manner, and nearly equal strength, are confused with one another. So of earlier painters, the name Guido da Siena seems to be merely a tradition of a much esteemed workman, whose exact date is variously given, and whose works cannot now be positively identified.

It follows that the ascription to a given painter of any picture, by internal evidence alone, is not an absolute assurance that it is entirely the work of his hand. Pupils may have worked upon it; and in many instances the most famous works of a master are those of which his pupils have painted the greater parts. This is wholly apart from true authenticity; just as, in a case where all the facts are known, Raphael was employing scores of assistants upon the Vatican frescoes, while Michelangelo, almost unaided, was painting the roof of the Sistine Chapel. Internal evidence can establish beyond reasonable doubt the relation of even a newly discovered picture to the early art of Italy; it can fix the school to which it belongs, its date, its resemblance to and divergence from well-known standards of art of that school and date; then its author, then the period of his life to which it belongs, and all this with a directness and a certainty of reasoning incredible to those who are not accustomed to the processes of technical and philosophic criticism. There are limits to this means of authentication; but it is the most judicious, unprejudiced, and satisfactory of all means. Even documentary evidence fails to tell whether the picture you see is as its painter left it; even signatures may be forged or altered; while skilled critical judgment fixes upon every brush-stroke that is not of the original work, directs its careful removal, rediscovers the picture of five centuries before, and judges it with a perfect willingness to disregard common tradition, and, if necessary, to go behind appended initials or dates.*

* See Vitet, "Etudes sur l'Histoire de l'Art," 3d series, (Paris, 1864,) for a detailed account of the evidence, and of the arguments pro and con., in the case of a fresco discovered at Florence in 1843, and now generally ascribed to Raphael.

NOTE.

In the following catalogue the names of the Italian painters have been arranged in chronological order, according to their times of greatest activity; except that some attempt has been made to group painters according to schools, whenever it could be done without contradicting too violently the sequence of time. Thus the first name is Giunta, the second Margaritone, the third Cimabue, and the fourth Duccio, and chronological order would require Giotto to come next; but Simone, though he both was born and died a few years later than Giotto, is put next to Duccio, because his immediate follower, and because representing a more archaic and less progressive school than that which Giotto was engaged in building up. The unknown painter of the Sienese altar-piece, No. 16, follows Simone; and thus, while the earlier Sienese form a group, Giotto and his followers are left in unbroken sequence, ten painters represented by sixteen pictures. The table on a folding leaf at the close of the volume, will be found useful, as by means of it the different schools can be readily compared.

The width and height of each picture are given in inches. These dimensions are of the painting itself, unless it is expressly stated that the frame is included.

Most of the pictures in the Jarves Collection are painted in *tempera*. This word denotes a glutinous medium—color mixed with glue, size, white of egg, or gum of some kind. The most usual Italian tempera was made with white of egg.

A few of the Byzantine pictures in this collection are painted in *encaustic*. This process, common among the ancients, consisted in painting with the colors mixed with wax, which previously had been dissolved in some way not now known, and in partly fusing the surface of the picture by heat, after the brush-work was finished.

Oil painting was not commonly practised in Italy before the middle of the fifteenth century. See the notice of Andrea del Castagno, page 53.

The four pictures by artists not of Italian schools are put together after the Italian pictures.

THE JARVES COLLECTION.

UNKNOWN PAINTERS.

(Pictures of the early revival of art in Italy—eleventh, twelfth, and thirteenth centuries.)

THE pictures numbered from 1 to 10, inclusive, belong to the dawn of modern civilization in Italy. This may be considered to begin with the eleventh century.

From the fifth to the tenth century had been a time of tumult and insecurity throughout Western Europe; and the tenth century was especially a period of intellectual decrepitude. Church-building, which in a barbarous fashion had been energetically pursued before, was then almost abandoned, and the fine and industrial arts were neglected. In Italy, the traditions of Roman and of early Christian art had been nearly lost. During all this period, Constantinople, under the Eastern emperors, was the centre of civilization. The tenth century seems to have brought with it, in the East, little of that dread which agitated Western Europe, of the approaching end of the world. Industry was better organized and more highly trained in the East than in the West. At this time "the subjects of the Byzantine empire were the most dexterous and diligent of nations; . . . and in the support and restoration of the arts their patient and peaceful temper was more useful than the warlike spirit and feudal anarchy of Europe."* In Constantinople were preserved some of the traditions of noble design and perfect execution of the Græco-Roman art under the earlier empire; and Christian symbolism, both before and after the short rule of the Iconoclasts, in the eighth century, was a favorite subject of study. Christian pictorial art gradually became, in Constantinople, formal, unvarying, and, to a great extent, a thing of rule and prescription; but its rules of design and technical execution, though limited, were sound; and it prescribed decorous, intelligible, and time-honored forms for representing the characters and events of Biblical and legendary religious history.†

The influence of the Byzantine example over the nascent art of the West is easy to trace. In Italy, the style of building and of architectural sculpture was and remained almost wholly European, taking but little inspiration from Byzantine practice, except in and near Venice. The energy of the Gothic and Lombardic races was more nearly one with the spirit of the

* Gibbon, chap. liii.

† A manuscript, probably of the tenth century, exists, in which are given exact rules for depicting not only each saint and sacred personage, but also many famous men of classical antiquity, and scenes and incidents, sacred and profane; also the best ways of preparing and using colors and other materials, and rules for painting every part of a church are exactly laid down. This manuscript has been translated into French by M. Didron, and published under the title "Manuel d'Iconographie Chrétienne," Paris, 1845. This must not be confounded with the same author's original work: "Iconographie Chrétienne, Histoire de Dieu," which has been translated into English, and published in London.

Franks than with that of the Byzantines; and the great and varied architecture of the North of Europe, even in the eleventh century, pressed upon the frontiers of Italy. But in pictorial art the Italians were more ready to learn of the Greeks; first, because the broad and unbroken interior wall-surfaces of the Italian churches required mosaic as their natural decoration, while the workers in mosaic all came from Constantinople; and, second, because there were many Greek pictures and miniatures in Greek manuscripts brought to Europe, which exceeded in technical merit and in grace of design any thing which the painters of Italy could find elsewhere.*

In short, though the Italian builders knew nothing of Byzantine building, they could build well themselves, in their own round-arched, *Romanesque*, or modified Roman way; though the Italian carvers occasionally saw Byzantine sculpture, and learned something from it, they found it too languid, and, moreover, had skill enough to carve and inlay for themselves their own restless and vivacious fancies; the Italian painters, however, were entirely mastered by the skill of Byzantine design, and the richness of Byzantine color.†

In different parts of Italy different influences were at work. In Rome, for instance, throughout the early Middle Ages, painters and priests (then often the same) seem to have striven to preserve or revive the

* Consult: Labarte, "Histoire des Arts Industriels," vol. iii.; Crowe and Cavalcaselle, "History of Painting in Italy," vol. i., *passim.*

† See below, in the notices of the early painters, and especially in the notice of Giotto, p. 30, further remarks upon Byzantine painting.

Roman traditions in their purity. But the Byzantine influence was generally triumphant. The great early painters of Italy—Cimabue, Giotto, Duccio, and their fellows—began as followers of the Byzantine laws, from the absolute authority of which they only little by little freed themselves. At Venice, archaic Byzantine pictures were still produced at least down to the time of the fall of the Eastern empire, (1453,) and, according to some authorities, until a later period; and in other parts of Italy.*

1. *Tempera, gold background, wood;* 14" *w.* 47" *h.*

Three compositions: THE CRUCIFIXION, THE DEPOSITION FROM THE CROSS, THE ENTOMBMENT. The architecture and costumes afford a means of deciding approximately upon the date of the picture, which, from this and other internal evidence, may be fixed as the eleventh century. It appears to be of pure Italian work, nearly free from foreign influence, and resulting from Roman traditions, held by monks in convents of Central Italy. The Y-shaped crosses are very remarkable; this form of the cross is almost unknown, and is certainly the rarest form known in Christian art.

This picture, without value as a work of art, is of great historical interest; the more so because works of this class are exceedingly rare.

2. *Encaustic, gold background, wood;* 5" *w.* 7" *h.*

THE NATIVITY. A purely conventional rendering of the subject, nearly of the character of miniatures in MSS. of an earlier time. As often in early works, the stable is represented by a cave, which in this case has a shed built over it.

* "The schools of painting founded by the Greeks in Italy lingered on, long after Giotto, strong in the affection of the populace."

"A Greek succession flourished until comparatively recent times in Otranto."—Lord Lindsay, "Sketches of the History of Christian Art," vol. i.

The boy in the lower left-hand corner symbolizes the adoration of the shepherds; and the angel above, the announcement of the Nativity to the shepherds. Inscriptions, as often in Greek pictures, are put over the heads of the personages; over the Virgin, ΜΗΤΗΡ ΘΕΟΥ, "Mother of God;" over S. Joseph an abbreviation of his name and title in Greek, 'Ο 'ΑΓΙΟΣ 'ΙΩΣΗΦΟΣ; over the angel Γ, for ΓΑΒΡΙΗΛ, "Gabriel;" over the shepherd Π̄, for ΠΟΙΜΗΝ, "shepherd," the horizontal line over the Π denoting abbreviation.

An unimportant picture, except for the rarity of such works in Europe; one of thousands executed by Grecian painters, or their Italian pupils, about the twelfth century.

3. *Tempera, gold background. A triptych, the centre 6" w. 9" h.; each wing 3" w. 9" h.*

In the centre, THE MADONNA AND CHILD, ATTENDED BY TWO SAINTS; on the spandrils above, TWO ANGELS. On the left wing, THE CRUCIFIXION; the Sun and Moon, in pictures of the Crucifixion, are generally supposed to represent an eclipse, as if to symbolize the darkness which covered the land, (Matt. xxvii. 45; Mark xv. 33; Luke xxiii. 44; Amos viii. 9;) they may also be taken to indicate the whole universe, watching the Crucifixion.* On the right wing, S. MICHAEL TRAMPLING ON THE DRAGON; below, TWO SAINTS, S. Dominic and probably S. Augustine.

This triptych seems to be Italian work, in bad imitation of the Byzantine manner.

4. *Tempera, gold background, wood. A triptych, the centre 15" w. 18" h.; each wing 7" w. 18" h.*

Nineteen compositions, forming a history of the Saviour and of S. John the Baptist. The key diagram will explain it: (1) THE ANNUNCIATION, (Luke i. 26;) (2) THE BIRTH OF CHRIST; (3) THE ADO-

1	17				18	
2	16		6		19	
3	15	14	13	11	10	12
4	5		7		8	9

* See Ruskin's "Stones of Venice," ii., 139, (London, 1853.)

RATION OF THE MAGI, (see under No. 15 for the legend of the Three Holy Kings;) (4) THE PRESENTATION OF CHRIST IN THE TEMPLE; (5) THE BAPTISM OF CHRIST; (6) CHRIST ADORED BY ANGELS; (7) THE LAST SUPPER; (8) THE AGONY IN THE GARDEN; (9) THE BETRAYAL BY JUDAS; (10) THE TRIAL BEFORE PILATE; (11) THE ECCE HOMO, (John xix. 6;) (12) THE SCOURGING OF CHRIST; (13) THE CRUCIFIXION; (14) THE DEPOSITION FROM THE CROSS; (15) THE ENTOMBMENT; (16) THE RESURRECTION; (17) S. JOHN BAPTIST IN THE WILDERNESS; (18) MARTYRDOM OF S. JOHN BAPTIST; (19) HERODIAS WITH THE HEAD OF S. JOHN BAPTIST.

Pictures of this kind were a convenient means of teaching to a people without books the events of the sacred history. They were meant to do for humble churches in poor communities what the great mosaics, like those of S. Mark's in Venice, did on a grander scale.

This triptych is of the twelfth century; it shows considerable originality in the conception and treatment of the subjects, but is very unskilful and barbarous in execution.

5. *Tempera, gold background, wood. An Altar-Piece,* 31" *w.* 72" *h., including narrow frame.*

The larger picture represents CHRIST AND THE MADONNA ENTHRONED, ATTENDED BY ANGELS. The Saviour holds a book, inscribed A.Ω., and, in the right hand, a sceptre. Above is a glory of cherubim (blue) and seraphim (red); this glory is continued below the feet of the principal figures, as if surrounding them. Below are also other angels, with musical instruments. In the gable above the arch is a small picture, representing THE OLD AND NEW DISPENSATIONS. On the right is the synagogue, or Judaism, represented as a blindfolded woman, holding a child in her arms; behind her an altar with sacrifice. The child may be meant to denote the partial, as if immature, truth held by the Jews. The personified Church stands erect and triumphant,* crowned, holding the sacramental cup, surmounted by the host or sacred wafer; behind her a baptismal font. An angel floats overhead bearing two scrolls, upon which are inscriptions. That over the head of the Church is, ECCE NOVA FACIO—"Behold, I make all things new," (Rev. xxi. 5.)

This is a most admirable specimen of the better Græco-Italian work. Its painter must have been a man of great ability, and highly trained in the Byzantine science and legendary learning. The picture is in fine condition; and it is especially interesting for having much of the grandeur and grace of a fresco, and a breadth of treatment rare in easel pictures of so early a time. It is of the beginning of the thirteenth century.

This picture is described and engraved in Fumigalli's "Museo di Pittura e Scultura delle Gallerie d'Europa," vol. xiii.

6. *Encaustic, gold background, wood; 7" w. 10" h.*

S. George Killing the Dragon. According to the legend, accepted during the middle ages, S. George was a Tribune in the army of the Emperor Diocletian; his well-known achievement took place in Phrygia; he afterward suffered martyrdom as a Christian. His death is said to have been in A.D. 326, and the peculiar reverence paid to him in the East dates back almost to that time. But in Europe he was little honored before the time of the Crusades. The inscription over the head of the saint in this picture is his name and title—'Ο 'ΑΓΙΟΣ ΓΕΩΡΓΙΟΣ.

7. *Encaustic, gold background, wood. A triptych; each part 6" w. 8½" h.*

[Nos. 7, 8, and 9 are parts of the same triptych, which has been taken apart for better exhibition. Five pictures, all of the same size.]

In the centre, Descent of Christ into Hades. The

* For the common mediæval contrasted representations of church and synagogue, consult Viollet-le-Duc, "Dictionnaire Raisonné de l'Architecture Française," article *Eglise.* See also Guenebault, "Dictionnaire Iconographique des Monumens," article *Synagogue.*

Church, in the Middle Ages, taught, as the Roman Catholic Church still teaches, concerning the good who died before the crucifixion of Christ, that they could not be admitted into Paradise, but inhabited a place called Limbus or Limbo, which was generally represented to be a part of or in the neighborhood of Hell, and from which Christ, at his resurrection, and before he appeared to his disciples, delivered them. An apocryphal gospel relates, amplifying the words of Matthew xxvii. 52, that some who had lately died were restored to life on earth, and that these related the scene of the coming of Christ, the defeat of Satan and [personified] Hades, and the release of those who were to be saved. In most instances the holy men and women of the Old Testament were held to be the only ones delivered, as in Dante's Inferno, Canto iv., where the just persons of pagan antiquity are left to a painless but hopeless eternity. In the picture under consideration Satan is represented as subdued and bound, with keys and broken chains scattered around him, while Christ raises and rescues those chosen to be saved. The Saviour's whole body is surrounded by an aureole, and his head by a cruciform nimbus, such as is worn only by the three persons of the Trinity. Upon the arms of the cross are the words, 'Ο 'ΩΝ, "He who is."

Over the head of Christ are the usual abbreviations of his name in Greek, ΙC̅ XC̅, and above this, again, the words, 'Η 'ΑΝΑΣΤΑΣΙΣ ΤΟΥ ΧΡΙΣΤΟΥ, "The Resurrection of Christ." The Descent into Hades is the second instant of the resurrection, of which the first is that usually represented—the coming forth from the sepulchre—and the third is the appearance upon earth to the disciples.

On the left wing, The Transfiguration. Around the form of Christ is a very curious double aureole—an oval intersected by an arrow-head, a very rare form. Above the head are the words, 'Η ΜΕΤΑΜΟΡΦΩΣΙΣ.

On the right wing, WANDERINGS OF THE ISRAELITES IN THE DESERT. On the right hand, Moses and the Burning Bush; below, the Camp of the Israelites, and in the left-hand lower corner, the Tabernacle. In the centre, Moses smiting the rock. Below, in front, the golden calf. In the right-hand lower corner, the passage of the Red Sea. In the centre, above, the giving of the law on Mount Sinai. On the right, above, the burial of Moses.

8. [*See No.* 7.] 6" *w.* 8½" *h.*

THE ANNUNCIATION, (St. Luke, i. 26,) in a purely emblematic form. The Virgin is enthroned under an architectural canopy, but seems to have risen at the greeting of the angel. The angel bears a stem of three white flowers, with red centres, (lilies?) and over his head is the inscription, ΓΑΒΡΙΗΛ, "Gabriel." At the top of the picture are the words, 'Ο 'ΕΥΑΓΓΕΛΙΣΜΟΣ, "The Good Message."

9. [*See No.* 7.] 6" *w.* 8½" *h.*

MIRACULOUS APPARITION OF SS. MERCURIUS AND CATHERINE. It is related that Mercurius was an officer in the service of the Emperor Julian, called the Apostate, and was put to death for adherence to the Christian faith; that he appeared to Julian during the tumult of his last battle, and threw the javelin which killed the emperor. In this picture he is represented as spearing the Emperor Julian, while S. Catherine is killing the Emperor Maxentius. The fallen emperors are represented as breathing fire, in sign of eternal punishment. See the figure of Satan in the centre of No. 7. Above is Christ, in the attitude of blessing. The names of the saints and of the emperors, in Greek characters, are put over their heads: 'Ο 'ΑΓΙΟΣ ΜΕΡΚΟΥΡΙΟΣ; 'Η 'ΑΓΙΑ 'ΑΙΚΑΤΕΡΝΙΑ; 'ΙΟΥΛΙΑΝΟΣ 'Ο ΠΑΡΑΒΑΤΗΣ, and ΜΑΞΕΝΤΗΟΣ. In the nimbus around the head of the Saviour are the words, 'Ο 'ΩΝ, and above is the abbreviated name of Christ, as in No. 7. On both sides of the head of Christ are the words, ΔΙΚΑΙΟΣ ΚΡΙΤΗΣ, "The Just Judge."

⁂ This small triptych of five pictures is an excellent and well-preserved specimen of the later Byzantine work, probably of the thirteenth century. Such pictures are rare in Europe, and are seldom met with in the picture-galleries.

10. *Tempera, gold background, wood;* 13" *w.* 17" *h.*

MADONNA AND CHILD. On both sides of the head of the Madonna are the abbreviations of ΜΗΤΗΡ ΘΕΟΥ, "The Mother of God." Late work, in the pseudo-Byzantine style, followed by the feeble thirteenth-century painters, whose abler contemporaries had created a new style for Italy.

GIUNTA DA PISA.

(Flourished about 1200–1255.)

Family name unknown. He signed his pictures Giunta Pisanus, or Junctus Pisanus. Said to have been born at Colle, near Siena; said by others to have been born at Pistoia, and to be of the noble family dall' Colle. Dates of birth and death not known. There is very little remaining of his authentic work; that little is mostly at Assisi and Pisa. His work shows some originality of conception, but is mainly Byzantine in character. If, however, recent criticism is right in dating the important pictures of Guido of Siena as late as 1270, Giunta is almost the first painter who appears as an independent and individual master.

11. *Tempera, on canvas over wood;* 38" *w.* 23" *h.*

THE CRUCIFIXION. Upon the uppermost arm of the cross is a label bearing the abbreviated Greek name of Christ, $\overline{\text{IC}}$ $\overline{\text{XC}}$; marking the Byzantine influence visible in every part of the picture. This inscription was replaced, in late Italian pictures of the Crucifixion, by the letters I. N. R. I., for Jesus Nazarenus Rex Judæorum; the inscription set up by Pilate, as given in John xix. 19. The head of Christ has a cruciform aureole; in the arms of this cross have been jewels, or enamels. The design is wholly conventional, the execution archaic and barbarous, and the surface has cracked in a way ruinous to whatever beauty the picture may once have had.

This picture formerly filled the head of a doorway in a church near Siena, for which place it was painted.

MARGARITONE DA AREZZO.

(*Circa* 1226—*circa* 1313.)

Family name not known. Pictures are signed Margarit de Aritio, or de Aretio. He was eminent as a sculptor and architect. His paintings have an archaic character, and many of the peculiarities of Greek design. As he lived at the time of the great advance in art under Giotto, (see page 30,) without sharing in it, he has been considered as the type of the earlier conventional school, and it has been generally believed that he angrily opposed all departure from the old forms.

12. *Tempera, gold background, canvas over wood. An Altar-Piece,* 64" *w.* 43" *h.*

Seven compositions. The subjects of them show the picture to have been painted for a chapel dedicated to S. Peter. In the centre THE MADONNA AND CHILD, WITH SS. LEONARD AND PETER, ATTENDED BY ANGELS; there are Latin inscriptions in Gothic letters, giving the names of the personages. On the left, above, CHRIST CALLING PETER. Second on the left, THE DESTRUCTION OF SIMON MAGUS BY SS.

PETER AND PAUL; the magician is the same spoken of in Acts viii. 9, 18, from whose name we get the word Simony. The legend is, that he appeared at Rome before Nero, apparently flying in the air, where he was supported by his subject demons, but that at S. Peter's command they let him fall. Below, on the left, S. PETER RELEASED FROM PRISON BY THE ANGEL. On the right, above, CHRIST'S CHARGE TO PETER, (Matt. xvi. 19.) Second on the right, THE HEALING OF THE CRIPPLE, (Acts iii. 2.) Below, THE MARTYRDOMS OF SS. PETER AND PAUL, which, according to the legend, were, S. Paul's by beheading; and S. Peter's by crucifixion —at his own request, and, because he felt himself unworthy to die as his Master had died, with his head downwards. Above each of the smaller compositions is a descriptive title in Latin, in Gothic letters.

GIOVANNI CIMABUE.

(1240—after 1302.)

His family name seems to have been Cimabue, but his family, which was noble, or at least of high rank, was called indifferently the Cimabui or the Gualtieri. He is said to have been led to study art by seeing Greek artists at work in Florence. His style, during the earlier years of his life, is Byzantine in character, but he introduced into his later works very important modifications in handling, and he deserves the reputation of having founded the truly native school of Florence. His greatest fame, however, is as the master of Giotto, (see that name, page 30.) His real strength is shown in fresco and in mosaic, as at Assisi and Pisa; small pictures like this, partly by his own hand and partly by his pupils under his direction, exhibit much of the old formalism of style.

13. *Tempera, gold background, wood ; 64" w. 22" h.*

MADONNA AND CHILD; SS. JOHN BAPTIST, JAMES, PETER, AND FRANCIS OF ASSISI.

DUCCIO DA SIENA.

(Flourished 1280—1320.)

Duccio di Buoninsegna was of Sienese family, the date of his birth is not known. Said to have signed pictures as early as 1278; earliest certain date, 1285, when he was employed upon important work. Latest date known, 1320. The Sienese painters, more than any others, preserved the Byzantine traditions, and, while using a skill and power of their own in the execution of their pictures, kept to the ornamental treatment and minuteness of parts which they inherited from the Græco-Italian painting. Duccio's work displays a power of drawing which was unrivalled at the time in Italy; and he may be looked upon as the first artist of modern times who could draw the human figure with approximate truth. But it is chiefly as a draughtsman that he excels his contemporaries, and his conception and treatment of subjects are not remarkably original. His labors were mainly confined to Siena.

14. *Tempera, gold background, wood; 22" w. 18" h., including frame.*

Two compositions: on the left THE CRUCIFIXION, on the right the MADONNA AND CHILD, ATTENDED BY ANGELS. These pictures are very remarkable to the student, because presenting an extraordinary truth and vigor of drawing, united with a touch and a manner of laying color not far removed from the later Byzantine work. This picture is in technical qualities not very unlike Nos. 7, 8, and 9, except in the skill, unequalled up to the time of Duccio, with which the gestures and drapery are arranged and the whole action expressed.

SIMONE MARTINI.

(1283—1344.)

Simone Martini, or di Martino, of Siena, known also as Simone Memmi. No family name appears. Martino was the name of his father; Guglielmo (William) was the name of his wife's father, abbreviated to Memmo; and he was called, indifferently, Memmi, or Martini. Signed his pictures Symon de Senis, and Symon Martini. Vasari calls him a pupil of Giotto, but this was probably not the case; he seems rather to have studied with Duccio,* or, as some say, with Jacopo da Torrita, the mosaicist;† and his work is certainly wholly Sienese in character. He is, indeed, the most perfect representative of the early Sienese school. His pictures are pure and bright in color, and rich with decoration stamped and embossed upon the gold background. The picture No. 15 represents his style and power much more nearly than a small picture generally represents the qualities of the work of an early painter.

15. *Tempera, gold background, wood. Wing of an Altar-Piece,* 18¾" *w.* 61" *h. over all.*

THE EPIPHANY, or Adoration of the Three Kings. Above, and forming part of the composition, THE ANGELS APPEAR-

* Crowe and Cavalcaselle, vol. ii., *passim.* Rio, "De l'Art Chrétien," i. 28 *et seq.*

† Rohault de Fleury, "Les Monumens de Pise."

ING TO THE SHEPHERDS. In the base, or *gradino*, two roundels contain THE ANNUNCIATION. The visit of the wise men, or Magi, to Bethlehem, (Matt. ii. 1,) is generally represented, in early legend and art, as in this instance. The story of the Three Kings of the East is entirely legendary. They are called Gaspar, Melchior, and Balthasar, and represented as respectively old and middle-aged and young. They are also taken to represent the people of the three continents, indicating the reconciliation of the whole world to Christ; and one of them is sometimes a negro. According to the legend, they were buried in Constantinople, whence their bodies were removed to Milan, in A.D. 320, and laid in the Church of San Eustorgio, which was built or enlarged to receive them. In 1162, Frederic Barbarossa removed them, and gave them to the Archbishop of Cologne; the famous Chapel of the Three Kings, behind the high altar of the cathedral, at Cologne, still contains their relics. This whole legend owed its great popularity to the fact that it was considered to symbolize the making Christ manifest to the Gentiles.

The picture contains in itself all the beauty of pale and shadowless color and graceful composition, which was the strength of the Sienese school; and shows much of the freedom of drawing which Duccio and Simone introduced. It is much more adequate as an example of Simone's than No. 14 is of Duccio's work.

The drawing for the upper part of this picture is preserved in the Uffizi, at Florence.

UNKNOWN PAINTER.

(Picture of the Sienese School, dated 1370.)

16. *Tempera, gold background, wood. An Altar-Piece of several compartments; 99" w. 96" h. over all.*

A monumental altar-piece from the suppressed convent of San Martino alle Selve, at Signa, near Florence.

The frame and pictures are one composition, and on the frame is the date 1370. In the centre, the Madonna and Child, enthroned, attended by angels, playing upon musical instruments. Above is a small circular panel. Christ, with the right hand raised in benediction, bearing a book inscribed A and Ω; on the left, SS. Albertus and Peter; and on the right, SS. Paul and Anthony. In small circular panels, on the left and right above, The Annunciation. See the same subject treated in a similar way in No. 15. The inscription on the frame cleared of abbreviations would read:

Sanctus Albertus & Sanctus Petrus Apostolus ‖ Anno Domini MCCCLXX, DIE XV. Aprilis ‖ Sanctus Paulus, Sanctus Antonius Abbas.

GIOTTO.

(1276—1336.)

Ambrogio (or Ambrose) di Bondone seems to have been his real name; the diminutive form of this Christian name is Ambrogiotto; but the immortal nickname, "Giotto," may be derived from other names as well, and Angiolo, Ruggiero, and Parigio have all been ascribed to him. He was born at Vespignano, near Florence, of a peasant family, and was a pupil of Cimabue, (see that name, page 26.) During his life took place a great advance in the fine arts, perhaps the most important that history records, and his own genius and devotion were in great measure the causes of the change. There is no artist of whom we have any knowledge, whose life and works give evidence of a more powerful and original genius than his. The contemporary and intimate friend of Dante, his work as an innovator in the formative arts may be fairly compared with the new birth of literature in Dante's poems. As an imaginative designer, uniting abundance and originality of conception with truth and vivacity of expression, he has probably never been equalled. In technical skill he was the first painter of his time; his only rivals in this respect were Duccio and Simone of Siena, (see above,) and the vast amount and varied character of his work made him in middle life supreme in this as in other things. All the stories of him indicate a flexible, many-sided, affectionate, and sympathetic nature; he was universally beloved, and wielded great influence, and, being employed in all parts of Italy and in France, the reform that he initiated was made general. His beautiful artistic life was worthily closed by the building of the unrivalled tower at Florence, still known as Giotto's Campanile.

His especial influence as a reformer in painting may be briefly stated as follows. The painting of his forerunners and contemporaries still retained many of the characteristics of Byzantine work,—traditional expressions of face and postures of body which the painter was hardly allowed to modify; a tendency to gloom and asceticism, shown in the character of these traditions themselves; colors generally dark and strong, allowing no relief or projection, without light or shade, and getting the necessary gradation by means of pure color, and the necessary brilliancy by means of burnished gold; a tendency to excessive minuteness and elaboration of parts, shown in the numerous sharp and thin folds of drapery, and the vigorously made-out patterns of stuff and embroidery. In building up from this foundation the fabric of Italian painting, Giotto did what Duccio did in part, and Cimabue sought to do. He gave to fresco the broad masses and pale colors it requires for its best effect; he rejected in all his work the undue influence of the miniaturists, simplified the parts of his pictures, rejected unmanageable detail, added light and shade, and indicated shadow; but more than all, he replaced tradition by observation, looked at the forms and actions of men, and took his faces, his expressions, gestures, dramatic action, all from nature.

He was not—the passing of sixty years and the energies of one man could not make him—so correct a draughtsman or so powerful a colorist as the great men of two centuries later; but his work was one of the greatest works that has ever been done by man, and his place is among the greatest men who have given their energies to art. It is necessary again to remind the student of art that the "easel pictures," small portable works, however interesting in themselves, but imperfectly represent the early painters, whose best work is always on walls of churches and palaces and only to be seen on the spot. The pictures in most of the great galleries of Europe ascribed to Giotto, however beautiful, do not enable one to estimate rightly Giotto's character or power.

The pictures, Nos. 17 and 18 of this catalogue, are unusually fine in many respects.

17. *Tempera, gold background, wood. A small Altar-Piece*, 29" *w.* 72" *h.*

THE ENTOMBMENT; the Madonna is clothed in purple, as is

usual in scenes of the sacred history later than the crucifixion, violet or purple being the usual color of mourning.

18. *Tempera, gold background, wood;* 13" *w.* 24" *h.*

THE CRUCIFIXION. The Father appears in the clouds in the attitude of blessing.

PIETRO CAVALINI.

Time of birth not known. Lived in Rome, and painted during the first forty years of the fourteenth century. A pupil of the brothers Cosmati, and, with them, founder of a short-lived Roman school. Giotto went to Rome about 1296, and found Cavalini there, who was probably older than he, but who seems to have worked under Giotto's direction, or as his assistant. The few remaining works of this artist seem to confirm Vasari's statement, that his style was modified by the influence of Giotto. He may be considered as the first of the Giotteschi, or followers of Giotto.

19. *Tempera, gold background, wood;* 50" *w.* 42" *h.*

THE ANNUNCIATION. The Father, represented as youthful, appears above the Archangel, and the dove passes from him toward the Virgin. The Virgin holds a book inscribed with the first words of her song of praise at the time of meeting St. Elizabeth, (Luke i. 46): MAGNIFICAT ANIMA MEA DOMINUM, "My soul doth magnify the Lord." The proper inscription would be: Ecce Ancilla Domini; but it is often omitted or changed.

TADDEO GADDI.

(Circa 1300—circa 1366.)

Probably a native of Florence. The last positive

date we have of any work of his is 1366, and he seems to have died soon after. Godson of Giotto, and for twenty-four years his pupil and assistant. Eminent as an architect, in painting he is overshadowed by Giotto, and, as many of his own works were carried out from Giotto's designs, his standing as a painter is hard to define.

Attributed to Taddeo Gaddi.

20. *Tempera, gold background, wood;* 18½" *w.* 15" *h.*

THE VISION OF S. DOMINIC. It is related of him that, while praying in St. Peter's Church, he saw, in a vision, SS. Peter and Paul, who gave him a book and a sword, and bade him go forth and conquer the world. This vision inspired him to found the great order of Dominican Monks.

Attributed to Taddeo Gaddi.

21. *Tempera, gold background, wood;* 29" *w.* 42" *h.*

S. JAMES, S. JULIAN, AND S. MICHAEL THE ARCHANGEL. On the aureoles, which are stamped and chased upon the gold background, are the names of the saints. S. Michael is generally accepted as the chief of the archangels, and, therefore, of all created beings. He is the captain of the heavenly host, and the conqueror of Satan. He is a very favorite subject of the early painters.

This picture has been ascribed to Starnina, one of the Giotteschi—a Florentine, who lived a little later than Gaddi. But there are no pictures which can be said with any certainty to be his, and his manner is not accurately known or recognizable.

UNKNOWN PAINTER.

(A picture of the school of Giotto; probably, from its warmer tone of coloring, by one of his followers in the northern part of Italy. Probable date, about 1325.)

22. *A large triptych; 61" w. 68½" h. over all.*

In the centre, the MADONNA AND CHILD; a goldfinch is perched upon the hand of the Madonna, and the child is playing with it. On the left wing, below, FOUR MALE AND TWO FEMALE SAINTS; namely, SS. Dorothea and Reparata, John Baptist, James, Anthony, and a Cistercian, who may be S. Bernard; on the right wing, below, the crucifixion. In the two half lunettes in the upper parts of the wings, THE ANNUNCIATION. Upon the frame are two shields, one bearing the arms of the now extinct Vecchietti family. The saints on the left wing are probably patron saints of that family.

This picture is in unusually perfect condition, and, although not to be attributed with certainty to any painter, is one of the most important pictures in the collection.

ORCAGNA.

(Circa 1315—1376.)

Andrea di Cione, of Florence, called L'Arcagnolo, (the Archangel,) a name which was corrupted into Orcagna, which last has remained his name in the history of art. He was the son of a goldsmith, and, like Francia, Pollajuolo, (see those names below,) and many other painters, first studied in the goldsmiths' shops. He studied afterward* with Andrea Pisano, a celebrated and powerful sculptor; and to his death Orcagna seems to have held the arts of painting and sculpture, and the compound art of architecture, more equally in his hands than any artist we have record of. He was a man of great and singular genius, more

* The assertion of M. Rohault de Fleury, ("Monumens de Pise," 179,) that he studied also with Agnolo Gaddi, seems unfounded, and is incredible.

dramatic and intense, though less equable and profound than Giotto, and the only worthy successor in the next generation of that artist, whom, however, it does not seem that he knew or had seen. In painting, his great frescoes at the Pisan Camposanto; in sculpture, the Shrine of Orsanmichele, at Florence; and in architecture, the "Loggia dei Lanzi," in the same city, are his best known works.

23. *Tempera, gold background, wood; 29½" w. 47" h., including frame.*

S. AUGUSTINE, in episcopal robes, with mitre and pastoral staff, and holding a book. S. LUCIA, bearing the palm of martyrdom, and the lamp, which is a peculiar attribute of this saint, considered as a symbol of the divine light. The names of these saints are on the frame below. Above, in roundels, are two evangelists.

⁂ This picture and No. 24 came from the convent of the Salvi, near Florence.

24. *Tempera, gold background, wood; 29½" w. 47" h., including frame.*

S. DOMINIC, holding a lily; S. AGNES, holding a lamb. The lamb is her attribute, as expressing meekness and innocence, and as alluding to her name; but, when the lamb has a cruciform aureole, as in this case, it is directly symbolic of Christ. The names of the saints are on the frame below. Above, in roundels, are two evangelists.

25. *Tempera, gold background, wood; 19½" w. 44½" h., including frame.*

S. JOHN THE BAPTIST.

26. *Tempera, gold background, wood; 19½" w. 44½" h., including frame.*

S. PETER. This and the one preceding are important pictures, in excellent preservation, and well representing the artist. Specimens of the work of the Giotteschi, equal to these in character and condition are exceedingly rare; few collections possess them.

PUCCIO CAPANA.

(Admitted to the guild of Painters, 1349.)

Dates of birth and death not known; a Florentine; pupil, assistant and imitator of Giotto. The works ascribed to him disagree in the evidence they give as to his ability and character as a painter. It may be assumed that many of them are not authentic. As a close follower of Giotto, his work would lack individuality.

Attributed to Puccio.

27. *Tempera, gold background, wood; 20" w. 42" h. over all.*

THE TRINITY, WITH SAINTS IN ADORATION. A mystical subject, often represented in pictures for private oratories. This picture, though archaic in style, is the work of an able painter, and shows firm and skilful handling. It has been much injured.

AGNOLO GADDI.

(1324—1396.)

Son of Taddeo Gaddi; lived in Florence, where he was much esteemed, but seems to have given himself to painting in the spirit of an amateur, and such work of his as remains is not of the highest degree of merit. Famous as teacher of Antonio Veneziano, (see that name, page 41.)

28. *Tempera, wood;* 13" *w.* 11" *h.*

S. Francis Receiving the Stigmata. S. Francis of Assisi, founder of the great mendicant order of monks called Franciscans, Minorites, Begging Friars, Capuchins, etc., is one of the most interesting figures in Mediæval history. The legend of him seems to assimilate his life as nearly as possible to the life of the Saviour, and one of the incidents is the infliction upon his hands, feet, and side of the wounds upon the body of Christ. It is related that shortly before his death, while praying, he saw in a vision the image of the Saviour on the cross, borne aloft by angels, and that he received the five wounds, those of the hands and feet being like nails beneath the skin, easily to be seen and felt, and that upon the side a cicatrice as from a lance-thrust.

UNKNOWN PAINTER.

(A picture of the school of Taddeo Gaddi.)

29. *Tempera, wood;* 15" *w.* 12" *h.*

The Agony in the Garden.

JACOPO DA CASENTINO.

(Was of middle age in 1350.)

Generally called Giacomo di Casentino. Dates of birth and death not known. One of the inferior Giotteschi. Vasari calls him a pupil of Taddeo Gaddi.

30. *Tempera, gold background, wood;* 20" *w.* 11" *h.*

Legend of S. Giovanni Gualberto, founder of the Monastery of Vallombrosa. The story will be found at length in Mrs. Jameson's "Legends of the Monastic Orders;"—the scene represented in this picture is that of Gualberto and the enemy he had forgiven going together into the church of

San Miniato on the hill above Florence, and the crucifix bowing its head in token of approval, a miracle which caused the repentance of Gualberto and his entrance into the religious life.

GIOTTINO.

An imitator of Giotto, and author of meritorious wall paintings in Santa Croce at Florence. His real name is not known. Ghiberti, the earliest writer who notices him, calls him Tomaso, Vasari calls him Tomaso di Stefano. Recent research has gone far to identify Giottino with Giotto di Maestro Stefano, who was painting in 1368. It is probable that works by more painters than one are given to "Giottino."

31. *Tempera, gold background, wood; 18½" w; 38" h.*

A tabernacle-picture. THE MADONNA AND CHILD ATTENDED BY S. JOHN THE BAPTIST, S. NICHOLAS DI BARI, S. DOROTHEA, AND S. REPARATA. S. Reparata rarely appears in art, except in early Florentine pictures. She was made patron saint of Florence in 680, and the former cathedral was dedicated to her; but the present cathedral and the city were put under the special patronage of the Virgin, about 1298. For the legend of S. Nicholas, see No. 62. In the arch above, THE CRUCIFIXION.

32. *Tempera, gold background, wood; a panel, apparently intended to fill a pediment above a larger picture, 28" w. 8½" h.*

In one composition: THE SHEPHERDS ADORING THE INFANT SAVIOUR and THE RESURRECTION. A curious and characteristic specimen of the landscape of the Giotteschi.

⁂ This picture is from the Rinucini Gallery.

SPINELLO ARETINO.

(Circa 1320—circa 1410.)

This painter, whose usual name as given above means Spinello of Arezzo, was a pupil of Jacopo da Casentino, but was an artist of greater power than his master. The smaller pictures generally ascribed to him are notably inferior to his larger works, and it may well be that the former were generally executed by his pupils under his direction, as was probably the case with the two pictures, Nos. 33 and 34.

In the manner of Spinello.

33. *Tempera, gold background, wood; 17" w. 24" h.*

THE CRUCIFIXION. Saints of later times are mingled with the holy women, and with Roman soldiers, who are the usual attendants upon this scene. Above is the Pelican, emblem of redemption by the blood of Christ.

In the manner of Spinello.

34. *Tempera, wood; 27" w. 12" h.*

Two compositions: on the left, THE VISION OF CONSTANTINE; on the right, FALL OF SATAN AND HIS HOSTS.

UNKNOWN PAINTER.

(A picture of the Sienese School, about 1350.)

35. *Tempera, gold background, wood. An Altar-Piece, 27½" w. 53" h. over all.*

THE ASSUMPTION OF THE VIRGIN. She is surrounded by an aureole in the shape of the Vesica Piscis, and upborne by adoring and singing angels. Above are cherubim and seraphim. The Virgin is clothed in white, to signify victory over death and sorrow. This mystic subject symbolizes the final resurrection and the union of the soul with the body.

Pictures of similar technical character in the Sienese Academy are attributed to Ambrogio Lorenzetti, the author of the noble fresco in the Town Hall of Siena.

LORENZO DI BICCI.

(Circa 1350—1427.)

There were three Bicci, father, son, and grandson, all painters of Florence. The works of the two elder Bicci are difficult to distinguish, and all are of secondary importance. (See Neri di Bicci, page 60.)

36. *Tempera, wood;* 28" *w.* 8½" *h.*

A votive picture in honor of SS. Cosmo and Damian, who were regarded as the helpers of the sick and the rescuers from danger, the patrons of physicians, and who were especially the patrons of the Medici family of Florence. The subject on the right is a common legend, which relates that they healed a man who had an incurable leg, by replacing it with the leg of a Moor who had just died. In the middle and on the left are incidents where their intervention saves from injury; probably these are the escapes in gratitude for which this picture was vowed, and was ordered from the painter.

ANTONIO VENEZIANO.

(Circa 1320—circa 1388.)

Antonio Longhi, a Venetian by birth, thence called Veneziano, seems to have left Venice young; was a pupil of Agnolo Gaddi, and became wholly Tuscan, and a Giottesco in manner. After the death of Orcagna, Antonio is the painter who best carried on the movement begun by Giotto. Of much less intensity, earnestness, and force than Orcagna, he was a master of the graceful design and pure and pale color of the school. His works are not common, and are of great interest.

37. *Tempera, gold background, wood. A small Altar-Piece,* 30½" *w.* 48" *h.*

THE DEPOSITION FROM THE CROSS.

⁂ Instanced by Crowe and Cavalcaselle, i. 491.

GENTILE DA FABRIANO.

(Circa 1370—1450.)

Gentile di Niccolo di Giovanni Massi, of Fabriano, a town in the mountain region of Umbria. A pupil of the Umbrian school, which was at that time under the influence of Sienese traditions, he developed his art in a direction different from that taken by his fellows. He resided for a time in Venice, but his later life was passed in Florence and in Rome, in which cities are his most important remaining works. One of his pupils was Jacopo Bellini, who was the father of Giovanni Bellini (see page 69) and of Gentile Bellini, who was named from his father's master. He was, therefore, one of the founders of the great Venetian school of painting, and his works in many respects resemble the later triumphs of that school.

38. *Tempera, wood;* 57" *w.* 15" *h.*

A painting on a chest, or cassone. There are five of these in the collection, all of great interest. These cassoni were chests which were made to receive the wardrobes of rich and noble brides; they were usually made with ridged tops, like gabled house-roofs; the tops gilded or covered with rich patterns, the front and two ends covered with pictures, the backs only plain. In one respect these pictures are of especial interest; they are generally of secular subjects, although of a time when art was almost entirely devoted to the service of the Church. They often contain, therefore, curious and instructive representations of the costume, architecture, and weapons, and of the manners and customs of their times. The modern interest in and study of the decorative arts of the past has brought these cassoni into great demand, and enormous prices are paid for fine specimens.

THE TRIUMPH OF LOVE. The following is from a minute description, in Italian, of this interesting picture.

"It appears certain that this lovely picture should be attributed to Gentile. It cannot better be described than by calling it the Triumph of Love. It is divided into two parts, with a doorway leading from one into the other. In the left portion, facing the spectator, is seen a pavilion, under which three graceful figures are seated, and, on the steps of the pedestal, another equally graceful figure is kneeling, in the act of supplication. This one, and the middle one of the other three, have arrows in their breasts, which have been shot by a little Cupid hovering in the air. The supplicant is a youth in love with the damsel, equally enamored with him, whom he demands from her parents. The satisfied expression and raised hand of one of them, as if to bless the union, testify that the demand of the lovers has been accorded. At the foot of the pavilion is a wood, and there, in an open space before the trees, is a dance of the guests assembled at the marriage-feast. Seated on the branches of a tree are two musicians, playing on the clarionet. All these figures are clad in tunics, over which are the long robes worn in the thirteenth century, which give majesty and decorum to the figures and to the entire scene.

"By this wood, through the aforesaid doorway, the Kingdom of Love is entered. The spouses are introduced into it by two priests of the Deity, one of whom is surrounded by rays. In the air, between the summit of two mountains—the dark representing sensuality, and the lighter color chastity—on a throne formed by two lions, on which he places his feet, seated on two black doves, is seen Love, with golden wings, a sceptre in his right hand, and a bow in his left. At the foot of the first mountain is Apollo chasing Daphne, who is being changed into a laurel; and on one side of the declivity of the same mountain are Venus and Mars, caught in Vulcan's net. Where the two mountains are united in the plain by their respective bases, rises in the foreground a beautiful fountain, throwing up its limpid waters to the throne of Love, and again falling in minute rain into an elegant basin, toward which Dante, Petrarch, and Boccaccio—who have sung so much and so well, in various ways, of this most captivating of human passions—are hastening on the left to quench their thirst. Dipping his right hand in the basin, and with the other shading himself from the rays of light, stands another figure, probably a painter, who, through the prism of the playful rain, is observing the marvellous effects of the same light divided into its seven colors.

"On the further side, other personages of great distinction are seen approaching the fountain, two of whom are crowned as sovereigns; and one, who is armed from head to foot, may possibly be Charlemagne, who, it is well known, often yielded to the shaft of Love; the other, a queen—probably Semiramis, 'who legalized impurity in her kingdom'—as though ashamed, turns her back on the spectators. These are followed by a warrior, also clad in iron, and crowned with laurel, leaning both his hands on the pommel of his sword, the point of which rests on the ground. Behind them are crowded together other figures.

"Lastly, in the background of the right-hand scene, appear the two spouses, escorted by the priests, pierced both of them by the same arrow, to demonstrate that they obey one soul-affection of mutual fidelity. The bride is then snatched over the mountain reserved for the chaste, as has been already stated, and conducted toward Love, in a chariot drawn by two stags with branching antlers, the symbol of eternity; and guided by the priest, in whom is observable the beauty of the soul, or of virtue, manifested by golden rays of light, and who is appointed to conduct true lovers to the happy kingdom of eternal Love. The forsaken husband, with uplifted arms, in vain attempts to follow her over the rugged pathway; and is therefore fain to turn his looks toward the chariot which bears away with it all his happiness, as though waiting for the moment to be reunited to her in a better world."

This picture is from the gallery of the Prince Conti.

39. *Oil, wood; 25" w. 37" h.*

MADONNA AND CHILD. The Madonna stands in a curious late Gothic niche or window, and supports the infant Christ, whose feet rest upon a cushion upon the parapet of a balcony. The building is slight and ornamental, and must be considered as a shrine, or as a painted frame to surround the figures. Roses and pomegranates twine around it. The picture is signed "GENT . . FABRIANO."

⁂ Crowe and Cavalcaselle (iii. 103) speak of this picture as "injured by restoring." When M. Cavalcaselle saw it in Florence, it was indeed entirely disfigured by repainting; since that time the new paint has been entirely removed; by great care and unusual good fortune this was done without appreciable injury to the picture, which is thus left in excellent preservation. The recovery of so admirable and characteristic a picture as this from the bad state it was in, is one of the triumphs of picture-collecting.

Gentile's pictures are excessively rare.

FRA ANGELICO.

(1387—1455.)

Born in Tuscany, died at Rome. His real name seems to have been Guido; but in 1407, upon entering the convent at Fiesole, he took for his monastic name Giovanni, (John.) He won the appellation of "Angelic" from the character of his life and works, and after his death was called "Beato," or the blessed. His full title then is, (as Lord Lindsay has said, iii. 154) "Beato Giovanni, detto Angelico, da Fiesole." His family name not known, his teachers not identified, nor is it clear whether he studied art before or after entering upon the monastic life. His chief works are in fresco, at Florence, Orvieto and Rome; they possess an altogether exceptional purity and sweetness.

40. *Right Wing of an Altar-Piece;* 18" *w.* 30" *h.*

Three saints; S. Zenobio, Bishop of Florence in the fifth century, in pontificals; S. Francis of Assisi, founder of the Franciscan order of monks, (see under No. 28,) S. Anthony of Padua, holding a flaming heart.

MASOLINO DA PANICALE.

(1403—circa 1440.)

Tomaso di Cristoforo Fini, said to have been born at Panicale, but now thought to have been a Florentine. The diminutive form of Tomaso is Tomasolino, and Masolino is an abbreviation of it. Pupil of Starnina, and probably of Ghiberti as well, he was a determined student of nature, and especially of the human figure, in the representation of which he gained a power of correctness far surpassing that of most of his contemporaries, and never equalled before his time. He would have been the leading painter of the first part of the fifteenth century, but for the altogether exceptional artistic power of his associate Masaccio. The two friends and fellow-workmen, both born within the space of one year, and both named Thomas, represent the nobler naturalism of the fifteenth century; as Paolo Uccelli and Fra Filippo represent, one the less dignified, abstract, and severe, the other the less thoughtful and more technical naturalism of the same era. Masolino and Masaccio are earlier, however, by twenty years than the others above named. Landscape painting takes a high rank in art, for the first time, in the works of the two reformers. Their work may be considered as the close of the era begun by Giotto, and as the beginning of a new time which ends in Raphael.

41. *Tempera, wood. A tabernacle-picture, with the arms of the noble family for whom it was painted. 20" w. 35" h.; and 39" w. 62" h. over all.*

THE MADONNA ADORING THE INFANT SAVIOUR, ATTENDED BY SAINTS. The background is a sweet and varied landscape, and in the middle distance are S. Jerome adoring the crucifix, S. John the Baptist, S. Francis of Assisi receiving the stigmata, and S. Raphael the archangel accompanied by Tobit. Above in the clouds, The Almighty in the attitude of blessing.

MASACCIO.

(1402—circa 1428.)

Tomaso di Giovanni di Simone Guidi, born at Castel San Giovanni, on the Arno, above Florence. He is often called from his birth-place, Tomaso da San Giovanni. The nickname by which he is more usually known is abbreviated from Tomasaccio, which is an augmentative, and of uncomplimentary force. Thus Maso being the Tom of the Italian Thomas, Masaccio may be translated, as Browning translates it, "Hulking Tom." * Masaccio is the most remarkable figure in the history of his time, a genius in art as original and as profound as any of which we have any knowledge. In technical skill, as draughtsman and as designer in color in a large scale, he anticipated the artistic triumphs of the sixteenth century. In reality of conception and in dramatic force, he was supreme over all the painters of his time. Masolino, (see above,) and he were the first painters who observed and portrayed men, animals, and landscape as they are in nature, and without the stiffness and unreality resulting from imperfect knowledge and skill. His work was as purely his own and underived as Giotto's, the fitting crown of a later time; and the greatness of Giotto's influence may be partly seen in the fact that, with only six score years between their times of greatest power, Masaccio's work was possible. The greatness of Masaccio, again, is seen in the fact that, with the crowd of artists succeeding him in Central Italy, of

* In "Fra Lippo Lippe." It is strange that so close an observer as Robert Browning, familiar, moreover, with early Italian painting in its highest significance, should have cared to take Masaccio out of his place in chronology and art, and put him thirty years later, among the followers of Fra Filippo.

This note affords an opportunity to call attention to the just and subtile comments upon Italian art, which are frequent in Browning's poems, as notably in Pictor Ignotus, The Bishop orders his tomb in St. Praxed's Church, Old Pictures in Florence, Andrea del Sarto, and Fra Lippo Lippi.

whom were the Lippi, the brothers Pollajuolo, Ghirlandajo, Perugino, and Verocchio, it is not until seventy-five years after his death—that is to say, until Signorelli and Michelangelo had reached middle life, and Andrea, Raphael, and Giorgione their full artistic development—that a power so well-balanced and harmonious is shown in the works of any painter, with the single possible exception of Leonardo, whose Cena is about ten years earlier. The solitary greatness in landscape which Mr. Ruskin has claimed for Masaccio—solitary until Titian and Tintoretto a hundred years later surpassed him—seems to be truly his. He died at twenty-six, with his power hardly developed and manifested in only a few works; but the art of Florence might well have been more truthful and sincere, and of wider reach and higher aims, in Andrea's and Michelangelo's time, if Masaccio had lived to middle life.

There are very few pictures existing which are to be attributed to Masaccio. That described below is of his early time.

42. *Tempera, wood;* 13" *w.* 17" *h.*

Infancy of S. John Baptist. The incidents at the time of the circumcision are meant to be represented — Zacharias and a woman conversing in dumb show; Elizabeth talking to another woman, and pointing to the child, as if discussing the question of his name, etc. (See S. Luke i.) In the background is a cistern of water, and the child, S. John, standing in it, supported by women—an incident, perhaps, symbolic of the life of the man who was sent to baptize with water. The picture has been very much injured, and has lost much of whatever beauty of tone it may have possessed. Freedom of action and gesture, unhindered realism of conception, and skill in drawing superior to its time, are still visible in it. It is one of the earlier works of Maso, who was a recognized painter at nineteen.

*** Supposed to have formed a part of the *predella* of the picture described by Vasari, in a chapel of the Carmine at Pisa.

PAOLO UCCELLI.

(1396—circa 1470.)

Paolo Doni, of Florence, pupil of the sculptor Ghiberti, and a leader in the school of natural incident, simple and cheerful subject, and brilliant design, which he did much to establish. He excelled in painting landscapes, buildings, and animals, and, from his supposed peculiar fondness for birds, took the name of Uccelli, or di Uccello. His most important remaining works are of secular subjects.

For remarks upon chest paintings, see above, No. 38.

43. *Tempera, wood. A chest painting; 58" w. 15" h.*

INCIDENTS FROM THE ÆNEID OF VIRGIL. This picture represents the adventures of Æneas, as related in the First Book of the Æneid. On the right, Juno descends to Æolus, and orders him to release the winds. In the centre, the vessels of Æneas are tossed in the storm, masts and rigging are carried away, and sailors washed overboard. The vessels have armorial bearings painted on their sides, as customary in Paolo's time. Around them are figures of the winds rushing out of the cave of Æolus; they are personifications of the winds known to the Italians by the proper names painted over their heads: PONENTE, LEVANTE, GRECO, MEZZODI, TRAMONTANA, etc. Farther to the right, Neptune appears, upon a lofty chariot drawn by sea-horses.

Two of the winds, ZEFIRO and EURO, (see the Æneid, i. 135,) are before him, as if rebuked. On the right, the ships have reached a harbor, and the crews are landing. Æneas and Achates meet Venus, dressed as a huntress, (verse 318.) Above, she appears again, as a goddess, (verse 405.) The names of Juno, Æolus, Venus, Æneas, and Achates are painted over their heads.

44. *Tempera, wood. A chest painting, and companion to No.* 43; 58" *w.* 15" *h.*

INCIDENTS FROM THE ÆNEID OF VIRGIL. This picture represents the further adventures of Æneas. On the left, he kills deer for his followers. (Æneid, i. 187, et seq.) In the centre is Carthage. Building is going on, with curious building-machines. The Temple of Juno (verse 446) is the most prominent building. Above are represented, as if on a high stage, the pictures from the war of Troy, which Æneas sees and remarks upon:

> "Quæ regio terris nostri non plena laboris?"

Beneath, the meeting of Dido and Æneas is represented. On the right is Rome, as the result of the wanderings of Æneas, with a tolerably faithful representation of the Pantheon and less accurate ones of Trajan's column, the castle S. Angelo, and other buildings, some of which are marked with their names.

DELLO DELLI.

(1404—circa 1465.)

Dello di Niccolo Delli, of Florence. A less known painter of the same school as Uccelli, with whom he was probably associated. Applied himself especially to decoration and the production of chest paintings, of which No. 45 is a good specimen. For an account of these, see above, No. 38. He is last heard of in Spain, in 1464.

45. *Tempera, wood. A chest painting,* 59" *w.* 16" *h.*

Tournament in the Piazza Santa Croce, at Florence. On the left is the front of the Church of Sta. Croce. Along the whole side of the square opposite to the spectator the windows are open, and are hung with rich stuffs and carpets. Ladies fill the windows, and look out upon the square. In the centre is the stand put up for the judges. In the foreground a board fence is put up, on the hither side of which are boys and men, some standing on benches to look over, some looking through chinks and knot-holes. On the other side of the fence the tournament is going on; two couples of knights are jousting; one knight, falling back, is caught by his squire. Other knights and squires fill the scene. Many of these personages are to be easily distinguished, not only by their armorial bearings, but by their names also, which are painted upon their dress or horse furniture. At each end of the lists are great banners. The details of armor, dress, and armorial devices are very curious. There are one hundred and forty-six figures in the composition.

46. *Tempera, wood;* 8" *w.* 11" *h.*

S. Martin dividing his Cloak with the Beggar. Martin was an officer in the imperial army, and serving in Gaul. Having given all he had in charity, and a beggar asking aid on a cold day, he drew his sword, cut his cloak in halves, and gave half to the beggar. The whole legend is well told in Lord Lindsay's *Christian Art,* and less fully in Mrs. Jameson's *Sacred and Legendary Art.*

ANDREA DEL CASTAGNO.

(1390—1457.)

Andrea di Bartolomeo di Simone, of a peasant family of Castagno, but resident afterward in Florence. An inferior artist of the Tuscan school, and an imitator of its greater masters. It is claimed for him that he was the first Florentine who practised oil-painting; and charged upon him that he murdered Domenico Veneziano, from whom he learned the secret, that he might enjoy it alone. There seems only questionable authority for either statement.

47. *Oil, wood; 22" w. 33" h.*

S. JEROME DOING PENANCE. See remarks upon this common subject under No. 60, below.

SASSETTA.

(Died in 1450.)

Real name seems to have been Stefano di Giovanni; also given as Christofano di Francesco. A painter who preserved in his work the manner of a much earlier period. Master of Sano di Pietro, and perhaps of Giovanni di Paolo as well.

48. *Tempera, wood; 15" w. 14" h.*

S. ANTHONY TEMPTED BY THE DEVIL IN THE SHAPE OF A WOMAN.

SANO DI PIETRO.

(1406—1481.)

Sano di Pietro di Mencio, of Siena. Pupil of Sassetta. The Sienese school at this time was far less advanced than the Tuscan. Sano di Pietro was one of the leading men of his time in Siena; his work preserved much of the character of the work of Duccio a century before. In Florence, at the same time, the improvement in technical as well as spiritual qualities begun by Giotto had been carried on steadily; and Masaccio, (see that name,) dying young in 1429, in Florence, had reached a technical skill nearly equal to that of Raphael. The work of Sano di Pietro may be compared with that of Simone Memmi, (see that name,) and resembles it much in purity and charm of color, in general gracefulness of design, and in almost total absence of shadows or shade, having all the characteristics of illumination in manuscripts. Sano is well represented by the two pictures in this collection; No. 50, in particular, is in his best style.

49. *Tempera, wood. Gradino of an Altar-Piece,* 72" *w.* 16" *h. over all.*

THE ADORATION OF THE THREE KINGS. (See the account of their legend, No. 15.)

The paintings upon the pilasters of the frame seem to indicate that this picture belonged to the chapel of some charitable fraternity.

50. *Tempera, wood. Altar-Piece,* 20" *w.* 26" *h. and* 28" *w.* 55" *h. over all.*

CORONATION OF THE VIRGIN. This a favorite subject for altar-pieces in chapels especially dedicated to the Virgin, who is thus distinguished as Queen of Heaven. Christ and the Virgin are enthroned; above is the Holy Spirit; a choir of angels attend, and around are many saints, among whom may be distinguished S. Peter, S. Francis, S. Augustine, and S. Margaret.

GIOVANNI DI PAOLO.

(Died after 1481.)

A Sienese. Was painting as early as 1423, and outlived Sano di Pietro, (see above,) under whose direction he seems to have worked.

51. *Tempera, wood;* 11" *w.* 8" *h.*

S. CATHERINE OF SIENA PLEADING BEFORE POPE GREGORY VII. THE CAUSE OF THE FLORENTINES.
Attributed to Giovanni.

52. *Tempera, wood;* 15" *w.* 8" *h.*

MARTYRDOM OF A BISHOP BEFORE A ROMAN EMPEROR.

UNKNOWN PAINTERS.

(Sienese pictures of the fifteenth century. They may be ascribed to the time from 1425–1450.)

53. *Tempera, wood;* 13" *w.* 18" *h.*

S. ANTHONY TORMENTED BY DEMONS.

54. *Tempera, wood;* 17" *w.* 12" *h.*

EVIL SPIRITS EXORCISED BY HERMITS. The demons appear in bodily form, as they are driven out, and the demoniacs clothe themselves in garments, which are brought by angels.

SQUARCIONE.

(1394—1474.)

Francesco Squarcione, of Padua. The name of his master is not known; but he studied with great devotion the remains of classical art, which at that time were attracting the attention of all Italy. The greatest men of his time—Masaccio, Ghiberti, Verocchio—were diligent students of the technical excellence existing in those remains which surpassed their own attainments ; but Squarcione devoted himself to the study of pagan antiquity as well as classical antiquity, as M. Rio has well said in another case, and became in after-life rather an antiquary than an artist. As a teacher, he enjoyed a widespread and lucrative popularity. His pupils were numerous, and among them was the more powerful and artistic Mantegna.

The valuable picture, No. 55, has been ascribed generally to Squarcione, but it has also been supposed to be by Mantegna; and it is not impossible that a further critical examination of the question may give the picture finally to the latter.

55. *Oil, wood;* 16" *w.* 25" *h.*

THE NATIVITY. Above the head of the Virgin is seen the vision of the shepherd. The Father appears above.

This picture was successfully transferred from panel to canvas, by Mr. John Howorth, of Boston, in 1867. (See also Nos. 64 and 75.)

MANTEGNA.

(1430—1506.)

Andrea Mantegna, pupil of Squarcione, (see above.) Squarcione was a successful teacher; his ultra-classicism itself was the means of benefiting his more judicious pupils, by surrounding them with the best models of antiquity. Mantegna, although the ablest painter of North Italy of his time, except the Venetian, Giovanni Bellini, was not the equal of the greater Florentines, his contemporaries. But as a painter of a northern Italian city, allied by his work with the rising art of trans-Alpine countries, and influencing at once Milan, where Leonardo was growing up, and Venice with her mighty school in its youth, he deserves especial study.

56. *Tempera, wood;* 15" *w.* 21" *h.*

The Crucifixion. The Virgin and S. John stand beside the cross. In the distance is a landscape and city.

MATTEO DA SIENA.

(1435—1495.)

Matteo di Giovanni di Bartolo, of Siena, succeeded Sano di Pietro as the leader of Sienese painting; but what has been said of the defects in the works of that school at the time, (see above, Sano di Pietro, and elsewhere,) is true of the painting of Matteo as well.

57. *Oil, wood;* 18" *w.* 30" *h.*

Madonna and Child, attended by Angels. The picture is noticeable on account of the rich details of costume and flower decoration.

UNKNOWN PAINTERS.

(Pictures of the Umbrian School, fifteenth century, and probably before 1450.)

The Umbrian School drew its inspiration from Siena as long as it remained isolated and independent; but it had no geographical centre, and the Umbrian painters who attained celebrity adopted the styles of more powerful schools. It is principally as an early influence upon such men as Gentile da Fabriano, Piero della Francesca, Giovanni Santi, and Perugino, that the Umbrian School is of importance.

58. *Tempera, wood; 26" w. 10" h.*

THE DEATH OF THE VIRGIN. Christ and the disciples surround the death-bed. Some are reading from the Scriptures, while he has just received into his arms, unseen by them, the soul of his mother, in the form of a new-born babe. This very archaic picture has been ascribed to Buffalmacco, but it is thoroughly Umbrian in character.

59. *Tempera, wood; 9" w. 13" h.*

Two subjects in one composition—S. JEROME IN THE WILDERNESS, and S. FRANCIS RECEIVING THE STIGMATA. For an account of S. Jerome, see under, No. 60. For an account of S. Francis of Assisi, see No. 28. His companion in this picture is his friend, the friar Leo, who is said to have witnessed the vision of the crucified Saviour from which proceeded the rays of light which produced the miraculous wounds. Above in the clouds is THE ANNUNCIATION, and below, a tablet with the dead Christ.

*** On the back of this picture are the arms of the Medici family.

FRA FILIPPO LIPPI.

(1412—1469.)

A monk of the Carmine at Florence. Entered the convent when a child, and seems to have been self-educated in art, studying the great works going on about him. He was a daring and powerful naturalist, and of the greatest energy and industry, second only to Masaccio in technical skill, and his worthiest immediate successor in Florentine painting. The stories about his profligacy and irregularities of life are as doubtful as are most of Vasari's anecdotes about the men who were not of his own time. What appears certain is, that he was a poor man, with poor relations dependent upon him for support or assistance, and that he was annoyed by debt, and poorly paid for his numerous works. See, also, the notice of Filippino Lippi, below, p. 71.

60. *Tempera, wood ;* 11" *w.* 18" *h.*

PENITENCE OF S. JEROME. Although this saint is often represented at study, and often as Patron in cardinal's robes, he is oftenest painted as the model of Christian penitence and victory over the flesh. He is then generally kneeling before a crucifix and holding a rough stone, with which he beats his breast. The lion is his constant attribute, and denotes partly the character of the saint and partly his solitary life in the desert. The subject is a favorite one with Fra Filippo. This picture, which is in fine condition, is more than usually, for a small work, characteristic of the master. It is a curious specimen of the landscape of the time. It has been said, in the notice of Masaccio, that he was the first painter who painted landscape from observation and with knowledge. The greatness of the innovation can be partly judged by observing the rock drawing in this picture, nearly contemporaneous with Masaccio's three frescoes in Florence, and by observing that the landscape even of Leonardo, fifty years later, is scarcely more realistic than this.

⁂ This picture formerly belonged to the Duke Cosimo de' Medici, and was hung in his guardaroba, (see Vasari's *Life of Fra Filippo,* and a note by the Florentine editors, who say that its fate is unknown.) Its companion picture, a S. Augustine, is now in the Uffizi gallery at Florence.

FRA DIAMANTE.

A Florentine, a Carmelite monk and companion of Fra Filippo, and his assistant in art. Very little is known of him. See notice of Fra Filippo, above, and of Filippino Lippi, below, p. 71.

Attributed to him, and, if by him, in his early manner, is

61. *Tempera, wood. A tabernacle-picture.* 21" *w.* 36" *h.*

MADONNA AND CHILD, ATTENDED BY SAINTS AND ANGELS.

NERI DI BICCI.

(1418—1486.)

Grandson of Lorenzo di Bicci, (see above, page 41,) a third-rate painter.

62. *Tempera, wood;* 9" *w.* 9" *h.*

LEGEND OF S. NICHOLAS, who is represented throwing gold through the window to save from infamy the daughters of a poor nobleman. S. Nicholas is an Eastern saint, but Bari, in South Italy, claims to possess his body, and he is generally called in Italy S. Nicholas da Bari.

BENOZZO GOZZOLI.

(1424—circa 1500.)

Benozzo di Lese di Sandro, called from personal characteristics Gozzoli, studied painting under Fra Angelico, and in youth preserved much of that master's peculiarly feeble and gentle style. In later life and with maturer power, he developed a wonderfully sweet, forcible, and natural art, but not of great dramatic power or religious intensity. His landscape backgrounds are among the loveliest of early art, his treatment of the human body and face natural and sincere; although his drawing is often feeble, his tone of color is bright and pure, and his pictures are full of light. His chief remaining works are a series of admirable frescoes on the walls of the Campo Santo at Pisa.

63. *Tempera, wood; 31" w. 31" h.*

THE ANNUNCIATION. Interesting as a perfectly representative instance of the treatment of this favorite theme by the better Italian painters.

ANTONIO POLLAJUOLO.

(1433—1498.)

A Florentine goldsmith. The two brothers Pollajuolo, (see the next notice,) belonged to the same trade, in which they excelled as designers, and their paintings show the same characteristics of sculpturesque design. They worked much together, and their works cannot always be distinguished. Antonio is the more powerful of the two, a vigorous anatomical draughtsman of the human body.

64. *Tempera, transferred from wood to canvas; 31" w. 21" h.*

HERCULES KILLING NESSUS; a well-known story of the Greek mythology. The background is an extensive landscape, the Val d'Arno, with Florence and Prato in the distance; the important buildings in Florence can be easily recognized, and it is evidently a view of the city painted from a distant point, a curious instance of early landscape-painting from nature.

The recent history of this picture is singular: when purchased for the collection, the figure of Deïanira was entirely painted out, the landscape and the body of the centaur being continued by later work, skilfully done. This was probably done during the time of Savonarola, the Florentine reformer, who, a few years before Pollajuolo's death, excited a religious and political agitation in Florence, attacked with especial earnestness art of mythological subjects and all representations of the nude form, and persuaded many painters to sacrifice their objectionable pictures and their studies of the naked model. The alteration in this picture may have been made by the hand of the artist himself. This addition was carefully removed, and the picture recovered in an almost uninjured condition. It was transferred from panel to canvas in 1867, by J. Howorth of Boston, very skilfully and with complete success.

PIETRO POLLAJUOLO.

(1443— .)

Brother of Antonio, (see above,) and outlived him. It is to be noticed of the work of both the brothers that it approximates to pure light and shade, with but little regard for color.

Attributed to Pietro.

65. *Tempera, wood. A Lunette,* 50" *w.* 11" *h.*

The Annunciation. Almost wholly a study in chiaroscuro. A great display of the author's knowledge of perspective, in his time a newly invented art, and exciting great interest.

VEROCCHIO.

(1432—1488.)

Andrea Cione di Michele, school of Donatello. An artist of wonderful versatility, but of such unrivalled power as a sculptor that he gave most of his attention to that art. As a painter, his work is more archaic than it should be for his time. His complimentary nickname, (Verocchio, true-eyed,) seems to have been inherited from his teacher, Giuliano Verocchio, but no sculptor before Michelangelo deserved it so well or reached so great general perfection.

Attributed to Verocchio.

66. *Tempera, wood;* 30″ *w.* 45″ *h.*

The Baptism of Christ. This picture is of the manner of Verocchio, but may be by one of his pupils.

LUCA SIGNORELLI.

(1441—after 1524.)

Son of Egidio di Ventura Signorelli, and born at Cortona. His master was Piero della Francesca, (see p. 65,) to whom he owed his style, which is never very strongly marked by the peculiarities of the Umbrian school, and which became in his maturity unique in vigor, dexterous rapidity, and free drawing of the human body. His faults are an excess of draughtsmanship, a certain lack of spiritual power as compared with his great technical skill, and too great harshness of contrasting light and shade. He is to be considered the forerunner of Michelangelo; in his age he gained some of that wonderful power of grand design of which Michelangelo is the great master.

67. *Tempera, wood; 17" w. 14" h.*

THE ADORATION OF THE MAGI. For the legend concerning them, see above, under No. 15.

⁂ This admirable little picture, one of the gems of the collection, is in perfect condition, and has never been cleaned, restored, or repaired in any way. It will need to be transferred to canvas at some future time, but will not be marred by that process, if it is rightly done. When purchased it had remained for many years, and probably ever since it was painted, in the Archbishop's palace of Cortona.

FRANCIA.

(1450—1517.)

Francesco, son of Marco di Jacopo Raibolini, and born at Bologna. Francia was the name of a goldsmith with whom Francesco was an apprentice; hence he was called Francesco di Francia, and often signed pictures merely "Francia Aurifex." He studied painting with Squarcione, but kept up his connection with his early trade, was particularly successful as a diecutter for medals, and is known to have signed his work of those kinds as "Pictor." He was one of the most important painters of the later fifteenth century. His work and that of Perugino may be well compared, as the latest specimens of the religious ideal painting, with the greater energy and range of Luca Signorelli, the most powerful of the naturalists of the century.

68. *Oil, wood; 18" w. 23" h.*

PORTRAIT OF THE PRINCESS VITELLI. The Vitelli family

were the lords of Città di Castello, in Umbria. They were destroyed by Cesar Borgia, in 1502, and their possessions added to the pontifical territory. The lady holds a rabbit, and wears a rich costume. The background is a beautiful landscape, evidently a study of the scenery in the neighborhood of Città di Castello.

This exceedingly valuable picture was obtained from the Giovagnoli family, who inherited it from the Vitelli, now extinct. It is in excellent condition.

PIERO DELLA FRANCESCA.

(Circa 1415—1500.)

Piero di Benedetto dei Franceschi, born at Borgo San Sepolchro, and often called, from the name of his birthplace, Pietro Borghese. A painter of the Umbrian school, (see pp. 57 and 63,) and pupil of Domenico Veneziano, but studied the more advanced art of Florence, made improvements in technical processes in painting, was employed in many cities of Italy, and, in connection with Perugino, (see next notice,) raised the Umbrian school to an important position. He seems to have taught or influenced Giovanni Santi, the father of Raphael.

In the manner of Piero.

69. *Tempera, wood. A chest painting.* 59" *w.* 17" *h.*

VISIT OF THE QUEEN OF SHEBA TO SOLOMON. A work of the highest rank of its class; one of the most rich and delicate ornamental paintings left us from the time of the Renaissance.

PERUGINO.

(1446—1524.)

Pietro Vanucci, called Perugino from the city of Perugia. Born at Città della Pievè, in Umbria, and studied at Perugia. He came to Florence at the age of thirty. He formed an independent style early in life, more matured and complete in design and technical qualities than that of any of the purely religious painters of the time, or any artists except three or four great Florentine naturalists. He brings the enthusiastic and single-minded devotion of the Giottesque school into the midst of the Cinquecento schools of more matured science, secular thought, and classical, often pagan, inspiration.

70. *Oil, wood;* 16" *w.* 21" *h.*

THE BAPTISM OF CHRIST. Above is the Father, surrounded by a glory of angels.

PINTURICCHIO.

(1454—1513.)

Bernardino di Benedetto, family name said to have been Biagi. His name, Pinturicchio, is a diminutive of *pintore*, "a painter." Worked as Perugino's assistant and under his influence, but clung more closely than his more versatile and popular, and more travelled associate to the traditions and practice of the Umbrian school.

71. *Tempera, wood. A painted waiter, twelve sided,* 26" × 26".

LOVE BOUND BY MAIDENS. An allegorical subject, from Petrarch's Triumph of Chastity. These decorated salvers, for the presentation of bridal or birthday gifts, were painted by the first artists, as, at a later time, the painted plates known as Majolica. This one bears the arms of the Piccolomini family, both on the front and on the back.

COSIMO ROSSELLI.

(1439—1506.)

Cosimo di Lorenzo Filippi Rosselli, pupil of Neri di Bicci, (see above,) unfortunate in his teacher, and contemporary with the far more powerful painters, Filippino Lippi and Domenico Ghirlandajo, so that he falls into a secondary position. An esteemed painter in his time, as appears from the large number of his pupils, among whom were Piero di Cosimo, Fra Bartolomeo, and Albertinelli, (see below.) His large wall paintings in the Sixtine Chapel, at Rome, and in San Ambrogio, at Florence, are important and valuable works.

72. *Tempera, wood; 26" w. 42" h.*

MADONNA AND CHILD, SUPPORTED AND ATTENDED BY ANGELS. A mystic picture in his early manner.

DOMENICO GHIRLANDAJO.

(1449—1494.)

Domenico di Tomaso Curradi di Boffo Bigordi, son of a goldsmith who was nicknamed "del Ghirlandajo," because of the garlands or wreaths (perhaps of silver filagree) which he made for the Florentine girls. The name descended to the son, Domenico, and to the grandson, Ridolfo, both able and famous painters. Domenico is "the great Bigordi" of Robert Browning's poem; he is a painter of great individuality, whose works show singular truth and simplicity of conception, a strong feeling for beauty of color and line, which preserves him from the affectation of archaism which ruined some of his contemporaries, sincere love of beautiful accessories and quaint landscape, and a power of drawing only surpassed at that time by the unrivalled Masaccio. Sandro Botticelli (see below) was Domenico's friendly rival; but from the works remaining of both painters, Ghirlandajo must be considered the superior, and, therefore, the first painter in Florence of his time.

73. *Fresco on tile;* 13" *w.* 18" *h.*

Portrait of a lady of the Tornaboni family. A head often introduced into his large frescoes, and supposed to have been his mistress.

SANDRO BOTTICELLI.

(1447—1515.)

Alessandro di Mariano Filippi, apprenticed in his youth to a goldsmith called Botticello, whence his usual name. Vasari seems to consider him the best painter of his time in Florence, but this could only have been in his youth; as he and Domenico Ghirlandajo grew up to their full strength, the superiority of the latter must have been recognizable. A not unworthy member of the extraordinary group of painters who worked side by side in Central Italy, from 1475 to 1525—an army of disciplined strength, the likeness of which in power, rightness and directness of aim, and purity of taste, all shared by so many men acting together, has never been seen since that era closed with the deaths, nearly simultaneous, of Signorelli and Perugino.

74. *Tempera, wood; 21" w. 33" h.*

MADONNA AND CHILD. The infant Christ holds a pomegranate, emblem of hope in immortality. Landscape background, with buildings.

GIOVANNI BELLINI.

(1426—1516.)

Born at Venice, son and pupil of Jacopo Bellini, who had studied with Gentile da Fabriano, (see above.) With this painter begins the record of the great Venetian school, which, adding Lombard and northern power to the Umbrian traditions, made neither expression of face, nor religious fervor, nor vigor of gesture, nor any one merit its especial aim; but sought to paint the visible world with perfect form, light, and color. Giovanni Bellini, however, had a religious solemnity of mind which influences all his work, and gives to his pictures a gravity of purpose which later work often misses. Throughout his long life he went on improving his style, and from his pupil, Giorgione, (see below,) learned much of the glory of color which is the especial charm of the Venetian works. The undoubted father of the most individual and unmatched school of painting of which we have any record—that which culminated in the work of Titian—his name is one of the most truly venerable in the history of art.

75. *Oil, transferred from wood to canvas;* 20″ *w.* 53″ *h.*

S. PETER. Landscape background.

⁂ This picture was transferred in 1867, by J. Howorth, of Boston.

UNKNOWN PAINTER.

(Picture of the Venetian school, circa 1430.)

76. *Oil, canvas;* 19″ *w.* 25″ *h.*

PORTRAIT OF POPE CLEMENT VIII.

GIORGIONE.

(1477—1511.)

Giorgio Barbarelli, a Venetian, and a pupil of Giovanni Bellini. His nickname, "Giorgione," is an augmentative, denoting his high stature and beauty of person. During his short life he exercised a great influence over Venetian painting. He is remarkable among painters for his peculiarly artistic rather than philosophical nature, and executive rather than emotional greatness. His observation of nature, and his conceptions of human character and of incident were wholly a painter's; his attention was given to the visible beauty of objects, in form, light and shade, and color; and, in men and women, rather to ideal beauty of aspect than to expression or action. He was one of the simplest and most unaffected of men and of painters, and his work is absolutely free from affectation and from morbid or excessive sentiment. As has been well said, the ascetic ideal had no charms for him; the ideal that he worshipped was the heroic ideal, the image of a glorified world, and of perfected men and women in the flesh.

77. *Oil, wood ; 31" w. 14" h.*
THE CIRCUMCISION OF CHRIST.

78. *Oil, wood ; 28" w. 26" h.*
PORTRAITS OF ANDREA GRITTI AND HIS SISTERS. This picture was painted about 1500, when Gritti was an admiral of Venice. He was afterward Doge, from 1523 to 1538.

BASAITI.

(Was painting 1470—1520.)

Marco Basaiti, or Baxaiti, born at Venice of a Greek family. Dates of birth and death not known. A painter of the school of Giovanni Bellini. His works are delicate in finish and exquisite in color.

79. *Oil, wood; 38" w. 24" h.*
MADONNA AND CHILD, WITH S. MARY MAGDALEN AND S. JOHN. Beneath are the portraits of those for whom the picture was painted, kneeling in prayer. Background a mountain landscape, with buildings.

FILIPPINO LIPPI.

(1460—1505.)

Pictures are sometimes signed Filippo di Filippo Lippi. He is said to have been the son of Fra Filippo, and pupil of Sandro Botticelli, (see those names above ;) but his style is certainly formed upon that of Fra Filippo, and he may have been his pupil rather than his son. His works are those of a true artist, his heads are fine, portraiture is constantly and beautifully used in his compositions, his color is richer and more developed than is usual in the Florentine school of his time, his love of delicate decoration and rich dress is very marked. He has not the highest dramatic power or religious intensity.

80. *Tempera, wood; 24" w. 50" h.*

S. SEBASTIAN. The arrows are treated merely as attributes; this picture, like most of those representing the saint, merely symbolizes the martyrdom. Above, an angel offers the martyr's palm and crown. In the background is a part of Florence, the tower of La Badia on the right. Dated 1479, and inscribed with the names of those who ordered the picture.

81. *Tempera, wood; 10" w. 13" h.*

THE DEAD CHRIST. A devotional picture, perhaps used for an altar-piece to a private altar, and has suffered from the smoke of candles. The face is sweet and refined.

PIERO DI COSIMO.

(1462—1521.)

Pietro, "the son of a cetain Lorenzo, a goldsmith," godson and pupil of Cosimo Rosselli, and always called by his name. A more able painter than his master, but injured by personal eccentricities, and by a striving to imitate the peculiarities of too many different masters. His later manner is partly founded upon that of Leonardo.

82. *Tempera, wood; 45" w. 21" h.*

THE STORY OF ACTÆON, who was changed into a stag by Diana, and devoured by his own dogs. In the picture his head only is changed. Three incidents of the story are represented in one composition: first, he discovers, by his reflection in a pool of water, the change that has taken place, and tries with his hand if the change is real; second, he seems to lament his fate; third, he is pursued and torn by the dogs. Very interesting landscape and animals.

83. *Tempera, wood;* 14" *w.* 10" *h.*

THE THREE ARCHANGELS, SS. Michael, Gabriel, and Raphael. Raphael is accompanied by Tobit. The donor is represented kneeling in the corner. Probably a votive picture.

LORENZO DI CREDI.

(1459—1537.)

Son of Andrea di Credi, and pupil of Verocchio. He was a fellow-student of Leonardo da Vinci, whose manner he closely studied and followed. He excelled as a painter in oil-colors, and his precise and careful handling, founded on Leonardo's surpassingly skilful workmanship, made him remarkable in Florence, where the broader style, caused by common use of fresco, more prevailed. Later in life his style was modified by the Florentine influence. His work is interesting, as being nearly always devotional in the spirit of earlier art.

84. *Tempera, wood;* 9" *w.* 12" *h.*

THE CRUCIFIXION. The background is a quiet landscape, with a town on the left, and on the right the sepulchre, with Mary approaching its door.

⁂ From a chapel in the Borghese Palace, at Florence.

In the manner of Lorenzo, perhaps by one of his scholars.

85. *Tempera, canvas;* 60" *w.* 30" *h.*

Two subjects in one composition—THE CREATION OF ADAM;

4

THE CREATION OF EVE. A repetition of the latter subject exists, in chiaro-scuro, at the bottom of the Annunciation of this painter, in the Uffizi Gallery at Florence.

FRA BARTOLOMEO.

(1469—1517.)

Bartolomeo di Pagholo di Fatorino, a Florentine, pupil of Rosselli and fellow-pupil of Piero di Cosimo and Albertinelli; became a monk. For a time, and after the death of Domenico Ghirlandajo, Baccio della Porta, as he was called, was the only painter of exceptional power in Florence; and he remained unrivalled by any Florentine, except by Andrea del Sarto, until his death. But the chief centres of painting had then been formed at Milan, where Leonardo lived and worked till 1519; at Rome, where Raphael painted from 1508 till 1520; and at Venice, where the best work was just beginning. Fra Bartolomeo succeeded in gaining something of Angelo's grandeur of design, and of Leonardo's surpassing dexterity, but his conceptions are not sublime, and his highest mental condition is a serene religious calm.

86. *Oil, wood. An Altar-Piece, 65" w. 76" h.*

A pietà: THE DEAD CHRIST IN THE LAP OF THE VIRGIN, AT THE FOOT OF THE CROSS. The feet supported by Mary Magdalen, the head by S. Dominic, whose features seem to be a portrait of Fra Angelico. The background is a broad and varied landscape; and there are represented two scenes in the history of the resurrection: Mary going to the sepulchre and finding it empty, the angel addressing her; and Mary meeting Christ, whom she mistakes for the gardener.

ALBERTINELLI.

(1475—1520.)

Mariotto Albertinelli, a Florentine and pupil of Cosimo Rosselli. A friend of Fra Bartolomeo, (see that name above,) and worked much in company with him. He had many of his friend's merits as a painter, but was irregular in his life and work, and a less able and exalted artist.

87. *Oil, wood. Half a door of a cabinet,* 22" *w.* 47" *h.*

The Archangel Gabriel. The whole composition was an Annunciation, but the door has been split in two, and the other half, with the Virgin painted upon it, lost or destroyed.

88. *Oil, wood;* 20" *w.* 25" *h.*

The Virgin in the Egg. A symbol of the predestination of Mary to be the mother of the Redeemer and the salvation of the world. This dogma became popular in the sixteenth century.

RAPHAEL.

(1483—1520.)

Raffaello Santi da Urbino, son and pupil of Giovanni Santi, who was a painter of merit. After his father's death he studied with Perugino, (see p. 66.) His early manner is founded upon that of Perugino, and is marked by the same religious abstraction, pure and somewhat feeble design, and pale and tender color. A certain originality appears, however, even in his early works, in which the somewhat conventional types of the Umbrian school are freely handled. In 1505 he visited Florence, and until 1508 was much in that city, studying the great paintings there, works of Masaccio, Ghirlandajo, Michelangelo, and Leonardo; associated in work with the purist and religious enthusiast, Fra Bartolomeo, and rapidly improving in technical skill. A sort of war was raging in Florence at this time, between the students of the classic art and followers of Michelangelo and the religious painters of the Umbrian school, led by Perugino, and numbering among them the few remaining followers of Savonarola. Raphael was recognized as belonging to the latter party, and became widely known as one who added to the simplicity and religious purity of the Umbrian school the vigor and directness of the great naturalists. His skill in representing nature was second only to that of Andrea del Sarto, (see p. 79;) the dignity and grandeur of his design were only surpassed by the finest work of Leonardo and Michelangelo; and these great qualities he brought to aid a religious enthusiasm almost equal to that of Fra Bartolomeo. At this point of his progress he was summoned to Rome, whither he went in 1508, and his earlier work there displays a better harmony between technical and expressional qualities than any before or after. If he had died at twenty-five he would have left the name of the most powerful and versatile of the earlier religious painters, and the greatest master of human expression in face and gesture, except Tintoretto, long afterward.

His work, after that time all executed in Rome, however remarkable and in some respects unrivalled, is weak in the central and most important quality, truth of conception. He was by nature rather a student of the science of design than an imaginative designer, but his early work is full of the simple impulse and energy of the early religious schools, and his true greatness is seen in its individual character and fulness of meaning. His later work, done to please a worldly priesthood and a thoroughly pagan court, is neither so simple nor so sincere. The influence upon him of the time and place was almost wholly evil, and he could hardly have remained the favorite painter of the Vatican, and yet have persevered in the way in which he had begun. His unsurpassed skill as a draughtsman, his unequalled power of representing human expression, and the peculiar grace and harmony of his lines, continue to be evidences of the singular art-power which was so often misapplied. The numerous pupils and followers, not having the strength nor the "transcendental" qualities of mind of the master, copied the weaknesses and the errors; so that his first picture painted in Rome—the *Disputà del Sacramento*—may be regarded as the turning-point, not of Raphael's life only, but of the great stream of central Italian art.

89. *Oil, wood; 22" w. 28" h.*

The Madonna, with S. John and Joseph of Arimathea, supporting the Dead Christ, in a solemn and simple landscape, with a distant view of the Hill of Calvary. The original design is by Perugino, and exists, in a fresco transferred to canvas, in the Albizzi Palace, Florence. This picture is attributed to Raphael, as being one of those which he copied or imitated from Perugino; and it is thought to be his earliest known work. It bears the marks of immaturity, with the pure ideality and religious sentiment which characterize the earliest efforts of Raphael, while under the influence of the Umbrian school alone, that is, before 1505. In several details of color and drawing, it is varied from Perugino's fresco; thus in the fresco, the Virgin and S. John wear shoes, and the drapery nearly covers the feet; the Virgin's eyes are closed, and she does not hold her girdle in her hand as in this picture; the waist-cloth is differently treated. The figures in this picture of S. John and the Virgin correspond perfectly with the same in the Crucifixion of Cardinal Tesch's gallery, now belonging to Lord Dudley, and painted by Raphael at the age of sixteen. The close tunic of S. John is alike in the two pictures, and has in both similar patterns of gold embroidery on the breast. The figure of Christ in the Crucifixion shows a great advance in power of drawing over the Perugino fresco and this picture on panel; and this latter must have been painted when he was not more than fifteen years old.

⁂ The picture is in excellent preservation. It was taken from a villa of the Chigi family, the head of which, in the time of Raphael, was the great banker of that name, his friend and patron.

LO SPAGNA.

(Circa 1485—circa 1530.)

Giovanni di Pietro. His surname signifies "the Spaniard," but it is not known whether he was born in Spain or not; as a painter he is wholly Italian. He first appears as a painter in 1503, and probably died about 1530. He is the most interesting and powerful, except Raphael, of the followers of Perugino. His early style is founded upon that of Perugino, very much as the early style of Raphael is; his later style is very like Raphael's, and pictures by him have often been ascribed to that more celebrated artist. Pictures from his hand or in his manner are rare.

90. *Oil, wood; 13" w. 20" h.*

MADONNA AND CHILD, ATTENDED BY S. JOHN AND OTHER SAINTS.

FRANCIABIGIO.

(1483—1525.)

Francesco di Cristofano Bigio was his real name. The more usual abbreviation of Francesco is *Cecco;* the appellation of Francia in this case may have another derivation. He was a Florentine, a pupil of Albertinelli, and early formed a friendship with Andrea del Sarto, (see below,) in partnership with whom he spent most of the active part of his life.

91. *Oil, wood; 32" w. 37" h.*

THE ADORATION OF THE MAGI.

ANDREA DEL SARTO.

(1487—1531.)

Andrea Vanucchi, of Florence, son of a tailor, as indicated by his surname, pupil of Piero di Cosimo. He joined with his fellow-pupil, Franciabigio, in opening a shop or atelier in Florence. His extraordinary technical skill, more especially as a draughtsman, won for him the title of "the faultless," "Andrea senza errore." He won the deserved reputation of being the best "*frescante*," or painter in real fresco, in Italy; and this because of the rare union of qualities he possessed, enabling him to paint at once upon the damp plaster, and without after retouching, pictures which were superior to the labored work of most other men. The circumstances of his life were unfortunate, and his own acts often foolish and even criminal. The conditions under which his work was done were heavily against him; and Vasari questions, as others have done, whether, in view of his actual achievements, it may not be supposed that he would have gained or deserved as great a fame as his contemporary, Raphael, if he had enjoyed the exceptional good fortune of that universal favorite. He had a power of drawing as great, and probably more natural and facile than Raphael's. He kept more of the religious spirit of the early work; his coloring never became chilled, and was never slighted, as in Raphael's later works. On the other hand, he nowhere shows those rare qualities of mind to which Ruskin, rightly calling them "transcendental," ascribes the great power of Raphael. It is probable that Andrea would never have reached the highest excellence. As a painter of the visible and actual, he would have been, under favorable conditions, unsurpassed in power, versatility, and truth; but he was without the mental and moral grandeur that would have made him a great imaginative painter, and his work shows nothing which can be considered equivalent to the solemn earnestness of Leonardo, the fervid, religious intensity of Perugino, or of Raphael, in his youth, or the balanced harmony of all pictorial qualities in the work of the great Venetians. See, also, articles on Raphael, (above, p. 75,) and Paul Veronese, (below, p. 87.)

92. *Fresco;* 20″ *w.* 27″ *h.*

MADONNA AND CHILD. The picture was almost destroyed when transferred from the wall to canvas, and nothing is left but faint indications of its former grace of design and sweetness of color.

UNKNOWN PAINTER.

(Probably a pupil of Andrea del Sarto, perhaps Puligo.)

93. *Oil, wood;* 22″ *w.* 28″ *h.*

THE DEAD CHRIST, SUPPORTED BY JOSEPH OF ARIMATHEA. The design is by Andrea del Sarto, and the work has many characteristics of that master's least admirable pictures.

SODOMA.

(1477—1549.)

Giovanni Antonio Razzi, or Bazzi. The name Sodona, also spelled Sogdona, seems to have been a family name, and Sodoma a corruption of it. He was born at Vercelli, in Piedmont. Early in life he settled in Siena, and became the undisputed leader of the Sienese painters of the time. The indigenous Sienese art, peculiar to the school, and independent of surrounding schools, was then in decay. Razzi took thither the art of Florence, as developed in Milan under Leonardo da Vinci, and himself became another Leonardo to Siena. As the chief of a long-famous and preëminent school of painting, he gained a reputation almost as general and as brilliant as Raphael's.

94. *Oil, wood;* 18″ *w.* 25″ *h.*

CHRIST BEARING THE CROSS. The man who is taunting him may be supposed the legendary Wandering Jew. The face of this personage has been injured by the religious enthusiasts of the time, in their rage against the offender.

95. *Oil, wood; 27" w. 39" h.*

MADONNA AND CHILD, ACCOMPANIED BY S. JOHN THE BAPTIST, S. BERNARDINO OF SIENA, AND S. CATHERINE. S. Bernadino carries a tablet bearing the letters I.H.S., his usual attribute. The correct derivation of this inscription is from the Greek word 'ΙΗΣΟΥΣ, "Jesus." S. Bernardino is said to have carried with him and given away cards and tablets bearing the sacred letters.

DOMENICO BECCAFUMI.

(1479—1549.)

Son of a laborer in Siena, and takes his usual name from his master, Lorenzo Beccafumi. He is called, also, Mecherino. He studied in Rome, and then returned to Siena, where he was the principal rival of Sodoma, (see above.) He studied and followed the style of Michelangelo.

96. *Oil, wood; 16" w. 22" h.*

S. CATHERINE OF SIENA SWOONING, supported by angels. She is dressed as a Dominican nun, and her hands and feet are marked with the stigmata.

RIDOLFO GHIRLANDAJO.

(1483—1560.)

Son of Domenico, (see p. 67,) and brought up and taught by David Ghirlandajo. Studied the manner of Michelangelo and of Leonardo da Vinci. Was disposed to imitate the latter. In the controversy that sprang up in Florence he took the side of Perugino, together with Raphael, Fra Bartolomeo, and Lorenzo da Credi, (see notices of those painters, above.) Raphael and he worked much together. When the former went to live at Rome, he left his work in Florence to Ridolfo, and afterward tried in vain to persuade him to follow to Rome. Ridolfo remained continually in Florence, where his beautiful and serene pictures were better appreciated than they would have been in the capital of the popes.

97. *Oil, wood. Lower part of an Altar-Piece; 81" w. 88" h.*

THE MADONNA AND CHILD, WITH S. JEROME AND S. DOMINIC. Landscape background, in which are different scenes and incidents, among them S. Jerome doing penance.

GIROLAMO COTIGNOLA.

(1475—1550.)

A native of Bologna, and pupil of Francia.

98. *Tempera, wood; 20" w. 26" h.*

S. SEBASTIAN. Two angels offer, one the crown, the other the palm of martyrdom.

JACOPO DA PONTORMO.

(1493—1558.)

Jacopo Carucci, born at Pontormo, in Tuscany, pupil of Ridolfo Ghirlandajo and of Andrea del Sarto. His youth gave promise of excellence, but he became one of the mannered imitators of Michelangelo. His works which remain are very unequal in power and merit. The picture No. 99 is of small value.

99. *Oil, wood;* 28" *w.* 28" *h.*

The Martyrdom of the Theban Legion, under the Emperor Maximian. The story is apocryphal. (See Gibbon, chap. xvi.)

100. *Oil, wood;* 19" *w.* 24" *h.*

Portrait of Cosmo dei Medici, Duke of Florence; died 1464.

CRISTOFANO DEL ALTISSIMO.

A pupil of Pontormo. Best known as a portrait-painter, in which capacity he was employed, says Vasari, by Cosmo dei Medici, first Duke of Florence.

101. *Oil, transferred from wood to canvas;* 17" *w.* 23. *h.*

Portrait of Amerigo Vespucci, in the costume of a magistrate of Florence, inscribed with his name.

UNKNOWN PAINTER.

102. *Oil, wood;* 22" *w.* 27" *h.*

Portrait of Dante—the commonly accepted likeness, which is taken from the cast made at Ravenna after his death.

UNKNOWN PAINTER.

103. *Oil, wood;* 18" *w.* 25" *h.*

Portrait of Fernando Cortez, with the inscription, "Ferd. Cortez Indor. Domitor."

SEBASTIANO DEL PIOMBO.

(1485—1547.)

Sebastiano Luciani, a Venetian and a scholar of Giorgione. He removed to Rome, where his works were much admired, and he became an assistant in some of the immense undertakings of Michelangelo. He seems to have understood the Venetian methods of painting, and to have followed them to his death. His religious pictures show little original power, and display the direct influence of Michelangelo. He excelled as a portrait-painter. He received great honor in Rome, and, after Raphael's death, was looked upon as the first painter there, as Michelangelo's attention was mainly given to sculpture. He received the office of *Frate del Piombo*, "Monk of the Signet," an honorary and almost sinecure office, the duty of which was to affix the leaden seals to papal governmental documents, and was called for the rest of his life Fra Sebastiano del Piombo.

104. *Oil, wood;* 19" *w.* 25" *h.*

PORTRAIT OF VITTORIA COLONNA.

MARCELLO VENUSTI.

(1515—1580.)

A native of Mantua. Resided in Rome, and was of importance only as a copyist of Michelangelo. His own works, not without evidence of natural gifts, are mannered and imitative; but in his time the art had become a minister to vanity, and a thing of great names rather than true things; so that copies after Michelangelo were preferred to the original work of less celebrated men, and Venusti, with others, copied him. One of his copies is of the immense "Last

Judgment" of the Sistine Chapel, and is now in the Museo Borbonico at Naples.

105. *Oil, wood; 16" w. 19" h.*

THE HOLY FAMILY, probably after Michelangelo's design.

GIORGIO VASARI.

(1512—1574.)

Born at Arezzo. A painter of inferior power, and a close imitator of the style of Michelangelo. He painted large pictures both in Florence and Rome. But his fame is not a painter's, but that of the historian of Italian art. He is the author of the delightful series of lives of the artists—"of the most eminent painters, sculptors, and architects"—which has been for so many years the principal source of all our knowledge of this most interesting and important subject. Recent research has shown many inaccuracies in his work, but its value as a living history, personal, anecdotical, objective, of the great revival of art in Italy, must always be very great.

106. *Oil, wood; 26" w. 32" h.*

THE DEATH OF LUCRETIA.

PARIS BORDONE.

(1501—1571.)

Of a noble family of Treviso. A student of both Giorgione and Titian. A painter of secondary power, whose work has much of the beauty of color, but little of the directness and force of design of the greater Venetians.

107. *Oil, wood; 17" w. 24" h.*

Portrait of Bianca Capello.

JACOPO DEL PONTE.

(1510—1592.)

Called Il Bassano, from his birth-place. An inferior painter of the Venetian school.

108. *Oil, wood; 16" w. 22" h.*

Portrait of Piero Strozzi, Marshal of France, and son of Filippo Strozzi, who opposed the Medici, and was called the Tuscan Cato, for his patriotism and voluntary death.

PAOLO VERONESE.

(1528—1588.)

Paolo Caliari or Cagliari; born and died at Verona, and generally known by the patronymic "Veronese," but spent most of his life at Venice. He visited Mantua in his youth and painted there; afterward made a short stay at Rome; but most of his work, after the age of twenty-five, was done in or near Venice. He was one of the most powerful and accomplished of painters. It is fortunate that much of his work remains; his immense pictures painted upon canvas have retained their freshness, and some of the most important have been removed to Paris, London, Turin, and Dresden; others remain in their original places; and although many have suffered from dampness and injury, and many have been entirely ruined by so-called restoration, there is much of his finest work in the perfect condition of painting which, having been rightly executed in the first place, need not fear natural decay.

The five great masters of the Venetian school are Giorgione and Giovanni Bellini, (see above,) of the fifteenth century; and, of the sixteenth century, Tiziano Vecellio di Cadore, known as Titian, Jacopo Robusti, called Tintoretto, and Paolo Veronese. Of this later triad Titian is the painter of the most equal and harmonious strength, both in conception and execution, in drawing as well as in color. Tintoretto's pictures display a wonderful originality of conception, and a depth and force of imaginative insight perhaps unsurpassed in the history of art; but as a painter he was unequal, and his pictures are sometimes disfigured by harsh color and exaggerated drawing; he is a man of wonderful genius, but a less accomplished artist than the unrivalled Titian. Veronese lacks something of Titian's senatorial grandeur of design, and something of his never-failing skill in drawing the human form, for there are pictures by Veronese in which the nude form has been imperfectly rendered; his color is less solemn and deep than Titian's, his composition less dashing and broad than Tintoret's. He is simple and unaffected in his style, a Giorgione of a later time and of greater accomplishments. His coloring is bright and pure, and so harmoniously united with an elaborate system of light and shade, that it may be doubted if anywhere in art this union of truth of color, truth of chiaroscuro, and truth of form has been so perfect as in the works of Paolo. He is a decorative painter in all his tastes, loves, as do all the Venetians, splendor of dress and of architecture, fills the backgrounds of his pictures with stately piles of pure Renaissance buildings of noble design, and delights in tracing the patterns of rich silk in and out of the folds of drapery. Not irreligious, for his is a grave and sincere nature, and no great Venetian was irreligious, he has yet none of the Florentine love of asceticism and of retirement from the world. On the contrary, there is in all his works a frank and confessed love of the beauty, power, and grandeur of the world, as he saw it in the lovely cities of Italy at a time when every building was a work of art, when dress was a means of adornment, and when for three hundred years a splendid system of decoration had been steadily developed to the culminating grandeur of his own designs.

He stands upon the brink of the precipice toward which art in the sixteenth century is hastening; his works show the tendency of the age toward allegorical conceits and paganism—away from facts and from Christianity; but his life and his works have virtue to save art from the fall which soon follows his death. Personified virtues and qualities, Faith, Charity, the Genius of Venice and the rest, have a living interest in his pictures, and a value which we are slow to believe possible. The pagan revival is to him, and in his pictures, a revival of the grace and of the poetic charm of Grecian fable, without the coarseness given it by its worshippers who surrounded him.

109. *Oil, canvas; 34" w.·41" h.*

THE CRUCIFIXION. The darkness that overspread the land, "from the sixth to the ninth hour," has been one object of the painter, and has given to the picture an unusual character of gloom. The figures are remarkably expressive of Veronese's treatment, and show on a small scale many characteristics of his life-size work.

Attributed to Veronese.

110. *Oil, canvas;* 24" *w.* 52" *h.*

CHRIST IN GLORY, WITH SS. PETER AND PAUL. A mystic picture of inferior value.

AGOSTINO CARACCI.

(1558—1601.)

The three Caracci—Ludovico and his two cousins, Annibale and Agostino—are considered the three founders of the Bolognese, or eclectic school. Agostino, however, was rather an engraver than a painter. The eclectics adopted theories of art before unknown, professing to take from each school and from each painter what was best in their work; they founded an academy, and first put practice of the fine arts upon its modern footing, as a sort of learned profession rather than a higher handicraft. Their influence upon painting was, in the main, evil; and especially so in respect to color. In Agostino's work, however, neither the strength nor the faults of the school are very forcibly shown. As an engraver, he stands well.

111. *Oil, canvas;* 60" *w.* 40" *h.*

VENAL LOVE. Cupid is breaking his bow in indignation. This picture is from the gallery of the Baron von Bodenfeld, where it was called a Titian—an instance of the reckless cataloguing of pictures, until lately so common, of which mention has been made before. It was engraved by Agostino, and published by Adam Bartsch in "*Le Peintre Graveur*," vol. xviii., under the title, "*Le Vieillard et la Courtisane*." The engraving differs from the painting in a few unimportant details.

GUIDO RENI.

(1575—1642.)

Born at Calvenzano, near Bologna. A pupil of the Caracci, and the ablest painter who ever followed the teachings of their school. He soon abandoned the mannered execution and gloomy color of the Bolognese, to search for a new style of his own, in which attempt he so far succeeded that he regained a freshness and purity of color unequalled by any of his contemporaries. He devoted himself to the pursuit of an ideal grace and sweetness, which he succeeded in representing in some single figures, and partly in a few of his large pictures. It is, however, only as an executant that he has attained any peculiar success; as an imaginative designer, he stands low; and whatever ideal of physical beauty he may have sought, his works show little care for any sacred ideal, and little capacity for religious enthusiasm.

112. *Oil, wood; 6" w. 10" h.*

JOSEPH HOLDING THE INFANT JESUS. This sketch is from the Gerini gallery of Florence.

113. *Oil, canvas; 65" w. 50" h.*

THREE GODDESSES DISARMING CUPID. Venus holds him, and the goddess on the right is Minerva; the one on the left, who has taken the bow, may be supposed to be Juno. A slightly painted picture, almost shadowless, and fresh and pleasant in color.

DOMENICHINO.

(1581—1641.)

Domenico Zampieri. Born at Bologna; died at Naples. A pupil of the Caracci, he became their most worthy successor, and carried their chosen style of painting farther than they had had power to carry it. He is the best draughtsman of the Bolognese school, and his design, though not to be compared with that of the greatest masters, has a certain air of physical grandeur, which has caused some of his more elaborate pictures to stand very high in popular esteem. His works have little elevation of sentiment, and are often disfigured by grossness and extravagance of conception.

114. *Oil, canvas; 35" w. 44" h.*

Artemisia, widow of Mausolus, king of Caria, who mingled the ashes of her husband with wine and swallowed them.

UNKNOWN PAINTER.

(A Picture of the Bolognese school.)

115. *Oil, canvas; 27" w. 34" h.*

The Madonna holding the Crown of Thorns.

SPANISH SCHOOL—DIEGO VELASQUEZ.

116. *Oil, canvas;* 49" *w.* 75" *h.*

FULL-LENGTH PORTRAIT OF A SPANISH GRANDEE.

GERMAN SCHOOL—ALBERT DÜRER.

117. *Oil, wood;* 11" x 11"; *circular.*

HEAD OF THE DEAD CHRIST.

GERMAN SCHOOL—HANS HOLBEIN.

118. *Oil, wood;* 12" *w.* 17" *h.*

PORTRAIT OF CHARLES V., EMPEROR OF GERMANY.

DUTCH SCHOOL—PIETER BREUGHEL.

119. *Oil, wood;* 17" *w.* 12" *h.*

THE PROCESSION TO CALVARY.

APPENDIX.

CONDENSED EXTRACTS FROM PREFACE AND DOCUMENTS PREFIXED TO MR. JARVES'S CATALOGUE OF 1860.

PREFATORY REMARKS TO THE CATALOGUE OF 1860.

DURING a long residence in Europe, chiefly in Italy, the writer was led to the study of art at large, the results of which, in the abstract suggestions, were given to the public in "Art-Hints" in 1855. The historical and critical researches required for the preparation of "Art-Studies," led to the conception of a gallery or museum of olden art for America, based upon a chronological and historical sequence of paintings, arranged according to their motives and technical progress. Without such a museum of reference, it was evident that a work on Italian art would possess but slight interest for our public; while, if formed, each would illustrate and add to the value of the other. Accordingly, he determined to attempt it. Familiar with Italian life; living in the midst of the art that was his daily study; in constant intercourse with many of the best European connoisseurs; assisted by sympathizing artistic friends, and particularly by a Greek artist, Sig. G. Mignaty, whose knowledge of the history and technical processes, combined with a keen perception and deep feeling in art, is very remarkable; after several years of search in the highways and byways of Europe—the writer succeeded in getting together the pictures described in this Catalogue, believing that ultimately they will be found worthy of forming the nucleus of a Free Gallery in one of our large cities, and thus be made to promote his aim—the diffusion of artistic knowledge and æsthetic taste in America.

In view of the very natural doubts and questionings which must arise in this country, where there exists no standard of comparison and but little critical knowledge of "old masters," there has been added to this Catalogue a series of documents, showing the estimation in which the collection is held by English, French, Italian, and American authorities. The weight of their joint opinions, to which others might be added, is, he trusts, sufficient to induce the public to give it their candid attention, without fear of being called upon to examine or enjoy works that are not *genuine*, and of the epoch and schools they profess to be. It should be kept in mind that, for several years, they have stood the severest test possible; to wit, the brunt of European connoisseurship in Florence, alongside of the most famous galleries known, where it has been a step from a "masterpiece" to some characteristic specimen of the same master in this collection. At the same time, the public must not expect to find in it those masterpieces which give reputation to the great painters; they are either fixtures in the edifices for which they were painted, or have been long since absorbed into the chief public galleries, and can never be seen in America. All that he proposed to get together, was *characteristic* specimens of the schools and artists that illustrate Italian painting, in a series which should, at a glance, give a correct view of its progress from A.D. 1000 to 1600—six centuries, embracing its rise, climax, and decadence. In no collection are all pictures of the same standard of excellence. So in this there will be found some that illustrate rather particular *motives* in art, with especial reference to its Christian inspiration, than any special technical excellence; it being part of his aim to show the topics most in vogue during past centuries. Further, the nomenclature is based upon the same system as that of the public galleries of Europe in general. But comparatively few pictures have undoubted historical pedigrees. For the rest, catalogues are the result of the best available criticism, based chiefly upon *internal* proof, sustained, where it exists, by collateral documentary evidence or trustworthy tradition. The author has conscientiously and studiously followed this system, aided by European criticism; and the Catalogue, as it now appears, is the result of several years' patient and close inquiry. Wherever he has felt there might be a diversity of opinion among critics, or he had any cause to distrust the evidence, it has been so indicated in the Catalogue; which, as a whole, will be found to be as correct as those of the galleries in Europe which are relied upon as authoritative.*

Several of the letters given among the "Documents" are addressed to Charles Eliot Norton, Esq. Mr. Ruskin, in a note to chap. viii., vol. v., "Modern Painters," writes of this gentleman and art-critic, "As I was correcting these pages, there was put into my hands a little work by a very dear friend,—'Travels and Study in Italy,' by Charles Eliot Norton. I have not yet been able to do more than glance at it; but my impression is, that by carefully reading it, together with the essay by the same writer on the 'Vita Nuova' of Dante, a more just estimate may be formed of the religious art of Italy than by the study of any other book yet existing. At least, I have seen none in which the tone of thought was at once so tender and so just."

With such a feeling for religious art, Mr. Norton no sooner heard of the writer's collection, than he wrote to him for information as to its destination, and to others conversant with it to ascertain its character; wishing to interest the friends of art in Boston in securing its permanent location there, with means to increase and perfect it. The replies are here appended, that they may have a wider circulation. Since Mr. Norton first brought the subject, in a private way, to the notice of his friends in Boston, the collection has been largely increased in number, besides receiving some of its most precious pictures.

JAMES JACKSON JARVES.

September, 1860.

* The Catalogue referred to is that of 1860; it contained the names of 143 pictures, some of which never belonged to Mr. Jarves, and were added to the collection for purposes of exhibition only. The first exhibition, for which that Catalogue of 1860 was prepared, was held in the Derby Gallery, No. 625 Broadway, New-York. The Catalogue of 1863, prepared for the exhibition of the pictures at the Historical Society's building, contained 134 numbers.

LIST OF DOCUMENTS.

I. Extract from the London "Athenæum," 12th February, 1859.

II. Letter of C. C. Black, Esq., of the "Science and Art Department," South Kensington Museum, London.

III. Letter of Sig. Bucci, Inspector of the Uffizi Gallery, Florence.

IV. Letter of Mons. A. F. Rio, of Paris, Author of "Life of Leonardo," and "Poetry of Christian Art."

V. Letter from Sir Charles Eastlake, Director of the National Gallery, and President of the Royal Academy, London.

VI. Letter of Louis Thies, Esq., Cambridge College.

DOCUMENTS.

I.

Letter of Mr. T. A. Trollope. From the London Athenæum of 12th February, 1859.

FLORENCE, January 20.

. . . .

I was invited the other day to visit a gallery of pictures, the collection and object of which interested me much, and seemed strangely to indicate the apparently inexhaustible artistic wealth which has been stored up in these old Tuscan cities, as in a garner, for the perennial supply of the entire world. They have furnished forth galleries for the delight and art-instruction of every nation of Europe; and now they are called on to perform a similar civilizing office for the rising world on the other side of the Atlantic. And to how great an extent they are still able to answer to the demand, the collection I am speaking of most surprisingly proves. It has been brought together by an American gentleman, a Bostonian, of the name of Jarves. One would have thought that it had been already too late to accomplish so patriotic a purpose, were not the gallery in question here to prove the contrary. English amateurs have wistfully sounded the owner as to the possibility of tempting him to relinquish one or two of his treasures. But the answer was, that the collection would go unmutilated to America.

This first attempt to make the New World a sharer in the

great art-heritage of Europe's old civilization is a circumstance so interesting, and, in view of the special bent the specimens obtained may give to an entire new lineage of art and artists, is so important, that it seems worth while to say a few words of the nature and merit of the collection.

Mr. Jarves has been for some years a resident in Florence, and has devoted himself entirely to this object. In the pursuit of it, Yankee energy and industry were, as a matter of course, not wanting. But the very creditable knowledge and judgment manifested in expending the funds devoted to the object, might, perhaps, have been less to be anticipated. But, most of all, the amazing good fortune which has helped him in his aim will strike those who can appreciate the difficulty of obtaining specimens of many of the masters.

Mr. Jarves has done wisely in seeking to make his collection especially illustrative of the history, progress, and, so to speak, genealogy, of the art; being aware that it is by such a study of its masters that an artist, as distinguished from an imitator, must be formed. He has also done well in paying particular attention to the condition of his specimens; preferring to have them with the mark of time upon them, when not such as to deface the master's sense and treatment, rather than to have more showy pictures at the cost of restoration amounting to repainting.

The collection is especially rich in specimens, one or two of them almost, if not quite, unique, of the earliest days of revived art. Some very curious Byzantine works of the tenth and subsequent centuries bring the history down to Margaritone da Arezzo, in 1240, who is represented by a most remarkable altarpiece. There is also a very important picture, as an historical document, of date between 1198 and 1216, which may be found engraved in the thirteenth volume of Fumigalli's "Collection of the Principal Pictures of Europe."

Cimabue, Giotto, Duccio, Taddeo and Agnolo Gaddi, Andrea Orcagna, Gentile da Fabriano, (a signed picture by this very rare artist, of whom not above eight works are known to be extant in Europe,) Fra Angelico, Sano di Pietro, Masaccio, (a fragment of a *predella* cited by Vasari,) Fra Filippo Lippi, Botticelli, Pietro Perugino, Lorenzo di Credi, Fra Bartolomeo, (a very grand altar-piece,) Leonardo da Vinci, (Holy Family, with same character of background and about the same date as Lord Suffolk's *Vièrge aux Rochers,* a very valuable and undoubtedly authentic work,) Lo Spagna, Sodoma, (two fine specimens,) Pinturicchio, Domenico, and Ridolfo Ghirlandajo, Raphael, (a very interesting early work, painted by him while still with his master, Perugino, from a design of his, but with variations,) all these, and several other less generally known names, are represented. There are also some interesting portraits, especially a contemporary one of Fernando Cortés; and a full-length Spanish grandee in armor, by Velasquez.

It will be admitted that no ordinary degree of good fortune must have been added to activity and judgment to render feasible the collection of such an assemblage of genuine pictures at this time of day. Those who have attempted, with more or less success, to purchase pictures recently in Italy, will probably be not a little surprised that it should have been possible; and it may be safely asserted that, if any other of the more wealthy communities of the United States, stimulated by the example and success of my Bostonian friend, should think, like Jack the Giant-killer's Cornish foe, " her can do that herself," and should attempt the feat with twice the pecuniary means, they will find that it is not to be repeated.

II.

Letter of Mr. C. C. Black, of the " Science and Art Department," South Kensington Museum, London, and for many years Agent of the Museum, for the purchase of works of art.

MY DEAR NORTON: July, 1859.

When Goldsmith laid down, as one of the two rules by which a reputation for connoisseurship might be attained, that the aspirant must praise the works of Pietro Perugino, we may presume he did not from any accurate appreciation he himself possessed of that old painter's merits, but rather that he selected the name as that of a recondite and rarely investigated luminary in the galaxy of Art. Keener eyes and better æsthetic telescopes have, however, of late years, been directed toward the pictorial sky; and Perugino's name would now stand far down, were we to catalogue the lights which shine from distances beyond the orbits even of Giotto and Cimabue, till the gazer is finally bewildered among Sienese nebulæ and Byzantine star-dust. These thoughts came on me forcibly, on crossing the Piazza Maria Antonia, after a by-no-means thorough examination of the very interesting collection formed by our friend J. J. Jarves. Although I think you visited it, when in Florence some years ago, his untiring energy has added to it so largely since you were among us, that I am minded to give you (without much pretence to chronological accuracy) some notes of a few chief objects of my admiration.

Though aware that Mr. Jarves had confined his purchases principally to the more ancient masters, proposing—and wisely—to illustrate the germ and growth of Modern Art, I was not prepared for the distance to which skill and patience have carried him back; and found him, to my surprise, the possessor of one of the earliest known representations of the Crucifixion, dating from the tenth, or possibly the ninth century. By the way, in writing to one who is acquainted with the galleries of the Catacombs, I may enter a *caveat* against the accusation of inaccuracy by explaining that I mean one of the earliest *movable* representations; excluding, of course, wall-paintings. Specimens of this date are naturally very rare: some, however, there are, and well authenticated; one, in particular, in the Museum of Fine Arts at Florence, closely resembling this of Mr. Jarves. A marked and distinctive peculiarity is the form of the cross; which, indeed, can be termed so merely for convenience, as it is Y-shaped, curiously resembling the embroidery on a priestly stole, and figuring, moreover, in the shield of the Archbishop of Canterbury. To step from this strange relic of early piety to Margaritone of Arezzo may not be strictly chronological; but, as I said before, this I do not profess to be. This old master is represented here by a Virgin attended by the saints Peter and Paul; the central painting surrounded with smaller ones, which show various events of their lives. Their martyrdoms, in particular, are packed with an economy of space truly wonderful. In singular contrast to the hard, rugged, Ben-Jonsonish energy of Margaritone, is a Greek painting of very early date, (well known to collectors, and engraved by Fumigalli,) highly finished in detail; the jewels of the tiara and the folds of embroidered drapery quite wonderful; but the features smooth, polished, and insignificant as one of Hayley's poems. I was much pleased with a small Giovanni di Paolo, representing a female saint in gray, who kneels to a pope. How these old artists caught the key-note of character in their figures! It seems as though there was in the childhood of Art something analogous to the actual childhood of human life; for even as an observant child unfailingly selects the chief characteristic, bodily or mental, of a visitor, so do we find these early painters insisting on distinctive character as determinately as though they had just been reading the "Ars Poetica." We have here a demure train-bearer and a sulky cardinal, both of whom I have seen in Roman processions —Corpus Domini, for instance—times without number.

Duccio, whose noble picture of Siena hangs on the Cathedral wall so awkwardly as to be hardly visible, may be admired here much more satisfactorily in a beautiful Virgin and Child, as also in a Crucifixion; showing what, to me, was a somewhat novel treatment of this much-worn subject. Perhaps no better example could be found, to show the soul these early masters put into their works, than the various expressions, gestures, and costumes here displayed on a space not larger than a sheet of letter-paper.

Fra Angelico appears here unmistakably in a painting of three saints—St. Zenobio, St. Francis, and St. Thomas, (I forgot which of them;) and an Adoration of the Magi, by Simone Memmi, would attract any one's notice, if only from a wonderful group of men, horses, and camels, thrust together in much-admired disorder.

I have really no time to expatiate on the various excellent specimens of painters, good and rare; such as, Pietro Cavallini, Andrea Castagno, Matteo da Siena—of whom we have a Virgin and Child, and happily not his oft-repeated and horribly elaborated Murder of the Innocents—Taddeo Gaddi, who shows us St. Dominic receiving at the hands of Peter the sword he used so ruthlessly against heretics. Nor can I do more than offer to more leisurely speculation two quaint Byzantine tablets, in which Julian the Apostate is being speared by Mercourios (?); while Maxentius undergoes the same fate at the hand, not of Constantine, but of one Dicaterina—St. Catharine, I suppose; but let it pass. I must, however, do homage to Sano di Pietro; an artist whose works, even in Italy, must be sought with care, as nearly all the best are confined to his native city of Siena. Nevertheless, we find here no less than three specimens of his handiwork—an Adoration of Magi; a St. Margaret, wonderful in drapery; and a Coronation of the Virgin, so pure and sacred in feeling as to show at once his right to the title of the Sianese Fra Angelico. Of Benozzo Gozzoli there is an Annunciation, in a state of preservation very uncommon; and the same subject by Credi, clean and fresh in coloring as all his works are, and treated in a very pleasing, unconventional manner.

"*Omnia ex ovo*," says the old physiological adage: and I presume that the Virgin Mary herself forms no exception to the rule. At all events, here we have the Virgin, very pleasingly painted by a scholar of Albertinelli, enclosed in an egg—not a *vesica piscis* glory, nor an oval mass of clouds; but a veritably well-painted egg—the shell broken open at the side, the fractured edges carefully drawn, so as to display the figure. Leaving unsolved the mystic meaning of this very pretty picture, I pass to another Virgin and Child, delicate in coloring and charming in expression, by Sandro Botticelli; and to a small panel, likely to be overooked by a casual observer, but very interesting, as being not improbably the identical Birth of St. John, painted by Masaccio, and described in Vasari. The circumstantial evidence, with which I shall not trouble you, is very strong in its favor.

You know the man of many names—Sodoma to the world,

Razzi of Siena to his familiars; and now, by favor of some of those confounded investigators, who upset our faith in Romulus Richard, Joan of Arc—nay, even would do so in respect to Shakespeare himself—Bazzi of Piedmont would seem to be the genuine name of the painter. Happily, these *rixæ de lanâ caprinâ* are very unimportant. The names may perish; but Romeo, Lear, Hamlet, and, though in humbler sphere, the Chapel of San Bernardino at Siena and the upper floor of the Fernesina at Rome, are undeniable facts. Mr. Jarves possesses a glorious Razzi—Christ bearing the Cross—almost as rich in coloring as the grand fresco in the Belle Arti at Siena, and decidedly nobler in expression—the point in which Sodoma was most commonly weak. A proof of this assertion may be seen by comparing his celebrated St. Catharine Fainting, in the Dominican Church at Siena, with the same subject as treated by Beccafumi in this gallery. Although in many points closely resembling, and generally to the advantage of Sodoma, the countenance of the Father, in Beccafumi's work, is far grander.

I should like to detail to you some of the gorgeous court-costumes devised by Paolo Ucello to grace the pageant where King Solomon, in all his glory, meets the Queen of Sheba; to speculate on the interpretation of a most perplexing and enticing allegory by Gentile da Fabriano, called the "Triumph of Love;" and to speak more fully than is now possible of a beautiful female head by Cesare da Sesto, of a soldierly Velasquez, of a large and important Ridolfo Ghirlandajo.

Before concluding this very imperfect review, in which I have left quite unmentioned many interesting pictures, let me revert to our old friend Perugino, with whose name I began my letter, and of whom Mr. Jarves possesses a small but unmistakably genuine painting; as also to our dearer friend Noll Goldsmith, whose other recipe was, "to observe that the picture would have been better if the painter had taken more pains." How very safely this remark may yet be applied to the Caracci and their school! Rarely, if ever, do we meet a work of the Bolognese school, which does not, in spite of its unquestionable merit, offend by a certain careless air, which seems to show that the painter felt himself fully equal, nay, possibly superior, to the requirements of his subject. On the other hand, the conscientious labor, the solemn purity, visible in every portion of a painting by Duccio, Fra Angelico, or Sano di Pietro, impress on us the conviction that these men felt called on to make a holocaust of the talent God had given them, in serving, as best they could, the Giver.

I must now conclude; and only hope that this imperfect summary may suffice to show what can be done, even at this late period of picture-hunting, when good judgment and activity are backed by patience and well-timed liberality.

C. C. Black.

III.

Letter of Sig. Bucci, Inspector of the Uffizi Gallery, Florence. Translated from the Italian.

Mr. Jarves:

Dear Sir: I have long been acquainted with your praiseworthy design of making, without regard to cost or trouble, a collection of paintings of our older Tuscan schools, in order to show how these masters prepared the way for the very excellent artists who lived in the sixteenth century, and to transport the same to America, to make known by examples in that remote region, just risen so high in the scale of civilization, the character of the primitive masters of art, and how they were able to make painting attain so eminent position.

However little the paintings of these masters may be appreciated by a people accustomed, for the most part, to the sight of works of mere illusion and pleasure to the eye, yet the paintings carried by you to America cannot fail of being of great benefit to artists, and institutions of education.

I congratulate you, Mr. Jarves, upon a selection, which, from its excellence, must have cost you much persevering research and money. Your politeness has enabled me, before your departure, to examine all your paintings; and among the number, by no means small, of excellent ones, permit me to especially notice, as very remarkable and rare, even among us, and of our own school, "The Rape of Dejanira," by Antonio Pollajuolo; that beautiful "Madonna and Child," by Sandro Botticelli; St. Girolomo, by Fra Filippo Lippi; the "Annunciation," by Lorenzo di Credi; the "Sacra Familia," by Lo Spagna, a scholar of Perugino; the "Holy Family," by Domenico Ghirlandajo; and a small and extremely rare and valuable picture of the "Adoration of the Magi," by Luca Signorelli.

Among later paintings of other schools, I admired a magnifi cent portrait by Diego Velasquez; and the "Crucifixion," by Rubens.

Permit me, then, before you leave our city, in attestation of my esteem, to contribute my feeble praise and congratulation for the efforts you have made for the advantage of art in your native country.

With, etc., etc., etc.,

EMILIO BUCCI,

Inspector of the Uffizi Gallery of Florence.

IV.

Extract of a Letter from Mons. A. F. Rio, of Paris, the well-known author of "Poetry of Christian Art," and "Life of Leonardo da Vinci."

You are quite right in trying to get pictures of the Sienese school, which has been, till now, less studied than the others, and which is growing more and more into repute. Your two pictures of Antonio Razzi (Sodoma) are quite sufficient to give an idea of that great painter, who has so often been compared with Raphael himself; but my weakness for the old school impels me to say, that, for my own gratification, I should prefer your pictures of Sano di Pietro. A time will come when that charming master will be appreciated to his full value, and his works sought after as so many precious gems of mystical thought. France, England, and Germany know him only by reputation.

I do not remember seeing a single picture of his in any of those countries. The specimen which you possess has two great advantages: it represents the painter's favorite subject—the Coronation of the Virgin—and is in a perfect state of preservation. I have observed in your collection a charming little picture by Matteo di Giovanni. Your Gentile da Fabriano is, on account of its date, an important document in the history of that school; and I should place still higher the Madonna between four Saints, by Lo Spagna, who was the best pupil of Perugino, next to Raphael.

You will render the science of art more accessible to those [in America] who cannot cross the seas to study it in its birth-place.

With the best wishes for the success of your patriotic undertaking,

Most sincerely yours, RIO.

V.

Letter of Sir Charles Locke Eastlake, President of the Royal Academy, and Director of the National Gallery. Died in 1866.

7 FITZROY SQUARE, LONDON, NOV. 16, 1858.

DEAR SIR: I rejoice to hear that you purpose to send your collection of specimens of early Italian masters, in its entire state. to America. Few would have taken the trouble you have gone through in discovering and obtaining these works. Your continued residence in Tuscany has enabled you to avail yourself of many excellent opportunities. Good fortune has also sometimes rewarded you; but to your discrimination and knowledge your success is chiefly to be ascribed.

I consider that the series in question would form an excellent foundation for a gallery of Italian art; and I trust that, in your native country, it will be appreciated and kept together. I purposely avoid particularizing any works, because I have at all times uniformly declined to give any kind of certificate as regards single pictures; but I can conscientiously congratulate you on the formation of the collection as a whole. I believe that many valuable additions have been made to it even since I saw it.

Wishing you all success in your patriotic object, I am, dear sir,

Your faithful servant,

C. L. EASTLAKE.

JAMES J. JARVES, Esq.

VI.

Letter from Louis Thies, Esq.

Mr. Thies is well known among connoisseurs in Europe and America for his successful exertions in getting together and arranging the Gray collection of engravings, lately bequeathed to Harvard University. Having been formed, without regard to expense, by the late public-spirited owner, it is the finest and most complete in our country, and is excelled by few only in Europe. Not only do we find in it the best impressions of the most celebrated engravers, but some of extreme rarity: one by Finiguerra, the father of Italian engraving, if not the European inventor, which is considered as *unique,* and would command a price that would startle the uninitiated in these matters. This collection is accessible to the student of art through the courtesy of the curator; and it does for the history of engraving that which I have sought to do for painting.

Mr. Thies, having devoted a lifetime to the study of art, with the advantages of a European education, is well qualified to speak on the subject. To an enthusiastic feeling for his pursuit, he joins the critical acumen and patient inquiry which distinguish his former compatriots, Rumohr, Kugler, Passavant, and Forster.

J. J. J.

CAMBRIDGE COLLEGE, Sept. 13, 1860.

MY DEAR SIR: I cannot help expressing to you the very great pleasure I had in being permitted to see, on several occasions lately, the specimens of the old Italian masters which you had the kindness to show me. I certainly never looked forward to seeing in America pictures of such great merit and value.

The Perugino—Baptism of Christ—is extremely characteristic of that master, and is one of his most pleasing compositions. The upper part—the Almighty with the angels—recalls to me Raphael's fresco in San Severo, Perugia, in which he borrowed this upper part from his master; only that, in your picture, the principal figure holds a globe instead of a book.

The Lorenzo di Credi Crucifixion pleases me still more. I think it is one of the most charming little pictures the master ever produced. The figure of the Saviour is wonderfully fine, and the expression of the Magdalen at his feet embodies the poetry of grief.

The portrait of the Princess Vitelli, by Franc. Francia, is a remarkable picture, most charming in the landscape. It is beauti ful in modelling, warm in color, and with those peculiar characteristics that please so much in Raphael's earlier pictures. The picture would be an acquisition to any public gallery, on account of the great rarity of the master, as well as for the subject.

Luca Signorelli is a still rarer master. Your specimen, the Adoration of the Magi, is as perfect a one as I have ever seen, and admirably represents the peculiarities of the artist. It is particularly valuable for its fine condition.

It would take too long to particularize all the pictures worthy of mention, even among those of your collection which you were able to let me see.

LOUIS THIES.

INDEX.

PAINTERS MARKED WITH A * ARE NOT REPRESENTED IN THE JARVES COLLECTION.

Agnolo Gaddi, notice of, 37.
———, school of, 41.
Agostino Caracci, notice of, 90.
Altissimo, (see Cristofano.)
Albertinelli, Mariotto, notice of, 75, mentioned, 67, 74, 79.
*Ambrogio Lorenzetti, mentioned, 41.
Andrea del Castagno, notice of, 53.
Andrea di Cione, (see Orcagna.)
Andrea Cione di Michele, (see Verocchio.)
Andrea Mantegna, (see Mantegna.)
Andrea Vanucchi, called Del Sarto, notice of, 79, mentioned, 49, 74, 76, 79, 80, 81, 83.
*Andrea Pisano, mentioned, 35.
Angelico, Beato Fra Giovanni da Fiesole, notice of, 46, mentioned, 9, 60.
*Annibale Caracci, mentioned, 90.
Antonio Pollajuolo, notice of, 61.
Antonio Veneziano, notice of, 41, mentioned, 37.
Aretino, (see Spinello.)
Arezzo, Margaritone da, (see Margaritone.)
Arezzo, Spinello da, (see Spinello.)
Authenticity of Pictures, 10, et seq.

Baccio della Porta, (see Fra Bartolomeo.)
Barbarelli, (see Giorgione.)
Bartolo, (see Matteo da Siena.)
Bartolomeo di Pagholo di Fatorino, (see Fra Bartolomeo.)
Basaiti, (see Marco.)
Bassano, (see Jacopo del Ponte.)
Bazzi, (see Sodoma.)
Beccafumi, (see Domenico.)
Bellini, (see Gentile.)
———, (see Giovanni.)
———, (see Jacopo.)
Benedetto, (see Piero della Francesca.)
Benozzo di Lese di Sandro, called Benozzo Gozzoli, notice of, 60.
Bicci, (see Lorenzo.)
———, (see Neri.)
Biagi, (see Pinturicchio.)
Bigordi, (see Ghirlandajo.)
Bolognese school, page 90, et seq.
Borghese, (see Piero della Francesca.)
Botticelli, (see Sandro.)
Breughel, Peter, 93.
Browning, Robert, mentioned, 48, 68.
Buonarotti, (see Michelangelo.)
Byzantine Influence, pictures showing, 19, (Nos. 3, 4,) 20, (No. 5,) 24, (No. 10, and Giunta da Pisa, No. 11,) mentioned, 26, 27, 31.
Byzantine Pictures, notice of, 17, et seq., mentioned or described, 18, (No. 2,) 21, (Nos. 6. 7,) 23, (Nos. 8, 9.)

Cagliari, (see Paolo Veronese.)
Capana, (see Puccio.)
Caracci, (see Agostino.)
———, (see Annibale.)
———, (see Ludovico.)
———, school of the, 92.
Carucci, (see Jacopo di Pontormo.)
Casentino, (see Jacopo.)
Castagno, (see Andrea.)
Cavalini, (see Pietro.)
Cimabue, notice of, 26, mentioned, 9, 18, 32.
Cione, (see Orcagna.)
———, (see Verocchio.)
Cortona, Luca da, (see Luca Signo relli.)
Cosimo Rosselli, notice of, 67, mentioned, 72, 74, 75.

*Cosmati, mentioned, 33.
Cotignola, (see Girolamo.)
Credi, (see Lorenzo.)
Cristofano del Altissimo, notice of, 84.
Cristofano, (see Franciabigio.)
———, (see Sassetta.)
Criticism of Pictures, 10, et seq.
Curradi, (see Ghirlandajo.)

Dello Delli, notice of, 51.
Domenichino, (see Domenico Zampieri.)
Domenico Beccafumi, notice of, 82.
Domenico Curradi di Boffo Bigordi, (see Ghirlandajo.)
*Domenico Veneziano, mentioned, 53, 65.
Domenico Zampieri, called Domenichino, notice of, 92.
*Donatello, mentioned, 63.
Doni, (see Paolo Uccelli.)
Duccio, notice of, 27, mentioned, 9, 18, 28, 29, 31, 54.
Dürer, Albert, 93.

Easel Pictures, 9.

Fabriano, (see Gentile.)
Filippi, (see Sandro Botticelli.)
Filippino Lippi, notice of, 71, mentioned, 59, 60, 67.
Fini, (see Masolino.)
Fra Bartolomeo della Porta, notice of, 74, mentioned, 67, 75, 76, 83.
Fra Diamante, notice of, 60.
Fra Filippo Lippi, notice of, 58, mentioned, 47, 49, 60, 71.
Fra Sebastiano del Piombo, notice of, 84.
Francesco Raibolini, (see Francia.)
Francesco, (see Piero.)
———, (see Squarcione.)
Francia, notice of, 64, mentioned, 83.
Franciabigio, notice of, 79.

Gaddi, (see Agnolo.)
———, (see Taddeo.)
Gallery Pictures, their relative value to Italian painting, 8.
*Gentile Bellini, mentioned, 42.
Gentile da Fabriano, notice of, 42, mentioned, 12, 69.
*Ghiberti, mentioned, 39, 46, 50, 56.
Ghirlandajo, (Domenico,) notice of, 67, mentioned, 49, 67, 68, 74.
———, (Ridolfo,) notice of, 82, mentioned, 83.
Giacomo di Casentino, (see Jacopo di Casentino.)
Giorgio Barbarelli, called Giorgione, notice of, 70, mentioned, 49, 69, 84, 86, 88.
Giorgio Vasari, notice of, 86.
Giottino, notice of, 39, mentioned, 12.
Giotto di Bondone, notice of, 30, mentioned, 8, 12, 18, 25, 26, 28, 33, 34, 35, 36, 37, 38, 41, 42, 47, 48, 54.
Giotto di Maestro Stefano, (see Giottino.)
Giovanni Bellini, notice of, 69, mentioned, 57, 70, 71, 88.
Giovanni di Paolo, notice of, 55, mentioned, 53.
*Giovanni Santi, mentioned, 65, 75.
Giovanni, (see Cimabue.)
———, (see Angelico.)
———, (see Lo Spagna.)
Girolamo Cotignola, notice of, 83.
*Giuliano Verocchio, mentioned, 63.
Giunta da Pisa, notice of, 24.
Gozzoli, (see Benozzo.)
Guidi, (see Masaccio.)
Guido Reni, notice of, 91.
*Guido da Siena, mentioned, 12.

Holbein, 93.

Italian Painting, compared with other schools, 9.
Italian style, early, 18, (picture No. 1.)
Italian people, disposed toward art, 10.

*Jacopo Bellini, mentioned, 42, 69.
Jacopo da Casentino, notice of, 33, mentioned, 40.
Jacopo del Ponte, called Bassano, notice of, 86.
Jacopo di Pontormo, notice of, 83, mentioned, 84.
*Jacopo da Torrita, mentioned, 28.
Jacopo Robusti, (see Tintoretto.)

*Leonardo da Vinci, mentioned, 49, 57, 72, 73, 74, 76, 80, 81, 82.
Lese, (see Benozzo Gozzoli.)
Lippi, (see Filippino.)
———, (see Fra Filippo.)
Longhi, (see Antonio Veneziano.)
Lorenzetti, (see Ambrogio.)
Lorenzo di Bicci, notice of, 41, mentioned, 60.
Lorenzo di Credi, notice of, 73, mentioned, 83.
Lo Spagna, notice of, 78.
Luca Signorelli, called Luca di Cortona, notice of, 63, mentioned, 49, 64, 69.

Luciani, (see Fra Sebastiano del Piombo.)
*Ludovico Caracci, mentioned, 90.

Mantegna, notice of, 56, mentioned, 56.
Marcello Venusti, notice of, 85.
Marco Basaiti, notice of, 71.
Margaritone da Arezzo, notice of, 25.
Mariotto, (see Albertinelli.)
Martini, (see Simone.)
Masaccio, notice of, 47, mentioned, 10, 12, 47, 54, 56, 58, 68, 76.
Masolino da Panicale, notice of, 46, mentioned, 47, 48.
Massi, (see Gentile da Fabriano.)
Matteo da Siena, notice of, 57.
Memmi, (see Simone.)
Mencio, (see Sano di Pietro.)
*Michelangelo Buonarotti, mentioned, 9, 13, 49, 63, 64, 74, 76, 82, 83, 85, 86.
Mosaic, 10.

Neri di Bicci, notice of, 60, mentioned, 67.

Orcagna, notice of, 35, mentioned, 9, 41, 42.

Paolo Uccelli, notice of, 50, mentioned, 47, 51.
Paolo Veronese, notice of, 87, mentioned, 80.
Paris Bordone, notice of, 86.
Perugino, notice of, 66, mentioned, 49, 64, 65, 66, 69, 75, 76, 78, 80, 83.
Piero di Cosimo, notice of, 72, mentioned, 67, 74, 79.
Piero della Francesca, notice of, 65, mentioned, 63.
Pietro Cavalini, notice of, 33.
Pietro Pollajuolo, notice of, 62.
Pietro Vianucci,)see Perugino.)
Pinturicchio, notice of, 66.
Piombo, (see Fra Sebastiano.)
Pisa, (see Giunta.)
Pisano, (see Andrea.)
——, (see Giunta.)
Pollajuolo, the brothers, mentioned, 49.
——, (see Antonio.)
——, (see Pietro.)
Pontormo, (see Jacopo.)
Puccio Capana, notice of, 37.
*Puligo, mentioned, 81.
Pupils, work of, 13.

Raffaello Santi da Urbino, (see Raphael.)
Raibolini, (see Francia.)
Raphael, notice of, 75, mentioned, 13, 47, 49, 54, 65, 74, 78, 80, 81, 83, 85.
Razzi, (see Sodoma.)
Reni, (see Guido.)
Ridolfo, (see Ghirlandajo.)
Rise of art in Italy, eleventh century, 15.
Robusti, (see Tintoretto.)
Roman school, early, 33.
Rosselli, (see Cosimo.)
Ruskin, John, mentioned, 19, 49, 80.

Sandro Botticelli, notice of, 68, mentioned, 68, 71.
Sandro, (see Benozzo Gozzoli.)
San Giovanni, Tomaso da, (see Masaccio.)
Sano di Pietro, notice of, 53, mentioned, 53, 55, 57.
Santi, (see Giovanni.)
——, (see Raphael.)
Sassetta, notice of, 53.
Savonarola, mentioned, 76.
Sebastiano del Piombo, (see Fra Sebastiano.)
Siena, (see Matteo.)
Sienese school, mentioned, 27, 29, 40, 54, 55.
Signorelli, (see Luca.)
Simone Martini, *or* Memmi, notice of, 28, mentioned, 9, 31, 54.
Simone, (see Andrea del Castagno.)
Sodoma, notice of, 81.
Spagna, (see Lo Spagna.)
Spinello Aretino, notice of, 40.
Squarcione, notice of, 55, mentioned, 56, 64.
*Starnina, mentioned, 46.
Stefano, (see Sassetta.)

Taddeo Gaddi, notice of, 33, mentioned, 37, 38.
*Tintoretto, mentioned, 8, 49, 76, 88.
*Titian, mentioned, 49, 86, 88.
Tiziano Vecellio di Cadore, (see Titian.)
Tomaso, (see Giottino.)
——, (see Masolino.)
——, (see Masaccio.)
Torrita, (see Jacopo.)

Uccelli, (see Paolo.)
Umbrian school, 42, 63, 65, 66, 75, 76.
Unknown Painters, 15, 29, 34, 38, 40, 55, 70, 81, 84, 92.

Vanucchi, (see Andrea del Sarto.)
Vanucci, (see Perugino.)
Vasari, (see Giorgio.)

Velasquez, 93.
Venetian school, 42, 70.
Veneziano, (see Antonio.)
———, (see Domenico.)
Venusti, (see Marcello.)
Verocchio, notice of, 63, mentioned, 49, 56, 73.
Verocchio, (see Giuliano.)
Veronese, (see Paolo.)
Vinci, (see Leonardo.)

Wall Painting, the good influence of, over Italian art, 9.
Wall Pictures, 8.

Zampieri, (see Domenichino.)

www.ingramcontent.com/pod-product-compliance
Lightning Source LLC
LaVergne TN
LVHW021423110826
845150LV00007B/2055

9781425508401